KT-418-868

Contents

About the author

Toni Battison is a trained nurse who has had considerable practical and teaching experience during her career working with older people and carers, including that of District Nursing Sister, Health Promotion Adviser, Health Lecturer for a Certificate in Health Education course and as the Manager of a small charity. She is now retired from the NHS and does some part time freelance work in the field of health information. Toni has written many publications promoting good health and is a regular contributor to local radio. She is an Associate Member of the Guild of Health Writers.

Toni has always been concerned about the need to support carers and patients to enable them to get the best from local and national services, as she believes that people obtain great benefit from being able to help themselves. While working for the Cambridge and Huntingdon Health Authority she helped create an information centre for patients and visitors at Addenbrooke's Hospital and, with other carers, started the Telephone Information Line for Carers of Elderly People, in the Cambridge area. She was joint winner of the Ian Nichol Prize for Health Promotion in 1990 and 1992 for these projects.

Toni lives near Cambridge with her husband and has three grown up daughters. She was the main carer for her mother (in her late 80s at the time of her recent death) and in the past helped her mother care for her father, following a series of strokes and epilepsy, until he died at home. Her experience in caring for her parents has given a personal perspective that complements her professional role.

Acknowledgements

The author thanks the many people – carers, friends and colleagues – who have contributed valuable help and advice throughout the production of this book. In particular:

Joni Grace, Community Mental Health Nurse, specialising in older people; Amelia Mustapha, Fundraising and Communications Manager, Depression Alliance; Staff members at Directions Plus, a Cambridge-based charity for disabled people and carers; Staff members at Lifecraft, a Cambridge-based self-help organisation run by users and ex-users of mental health services.

Staff members at Age Concern England who were particularly helpful include Richard Holloway, Vinnette Marshall and Sue Henning, while Richenda Milton-Thompson worked on the manuscript in a freelance editorial capacity.

A number of people, some of them unknown to me, reviewed the draft material and made important suggestions to help improve the text.

In addition I thank all the national organisations that offer information and support to carers in the broadest sense, whose materials have helped to inform and influence my thinking.

Toni Battison

Introduction

Older people have many challenges to face. Just getting older is difficult enough, but people of advancing years are more likely to experience physical illness or the death of a friend or family member than when they were younger. These kind of stressful or difficult events can contribute towards an episode of depression. Despite this, depression is not just a 'normal part' of getting older. It is an illness which most people will recover from if given the appropriate treatment.

The word 'depression' is used to describe everyday feelings of low mood which affect us all from time to time. If someone is affected by clinical depression then they have an illness and this book will help you to identify the symptoms. Often people will not recognise that they are ill, or if they suspect that something is wrong, will refuse to seek help, mistakenly believing that depression is a weakness and that they shouldn't bother their doctor with anything but a physical illness. It often falls to friends and family to acknowledge the signs and encourage the person concerned to seek treatment. This can be an incredibly difficult task as depression is much misunderstood, and naturally people are afraid of what will happen once they have been diagnosed. This book will guide you through recognising depression and providing support to someone affected by it. It contains many useful facts to help dispel the myths and misunderstandings which make the condition so terrifying.

It can be very difficult when someone you care about is depressed. They need your support, but sometimes can't be affectionate or thank you for your concern. This can make being patient and loving difficult. Talking about sad feelings can be very beneficial for someone who is depressed and being a good listener is as important as providing practical help with the everyday chores that they may no longer be able to cope with themselves. Providing all that support can take its toll on a person's health and this book will provide you with useful advice on how to look after someone with depression whilst taking care of your own health.

No-one should fear depression; the vast majority of people affected will make a full recovery after appropriate treatment, and many find that the experience forces them to make some positive changes to their lives. Unfortunately, during a bout of the illness it is very hard to see the light at the end of the tunnel. This book will guide you through the journey and arm you with the knowledge needed to fight the condition every step of the way.

Amelia Mustapha
Fundraising and Communications Manager
Depression Alliance

1 What does being 'depressed' mean?

It is a rare person who can say 'I have never felt depressed' because depression in one form or another is very common. But while levels of depression vary enormously, so too does the point at which people recognise their symptoms or admit to feeling low. Whether or not these symptoms are severe enough to be diagnosed as 'depressive illness', most people acknowledge that some days are less good than others. We tend to describe these dips in mood in terms such as: 'I feel low' or, 'I'm having one of my down days'. Our bodies may also give off signals that actually make us look 'deflated' – a lowered head or glum expression send out a definite message to people around us that the effort of smiling or being sociable is just too much for us to cope with.

However, it is important to understand that there is a very clear distinction between the everyday 'feelings of depression', which tend to be used to describe a low frame of mind, and the medical term which refers to a clinical illness. In other words, feeling mildly 'blue' with a 'depressed' mood is different to actually suffering from depression.

Depression, as an illness, is one of the most common disorders in the UK, affecting about one in five people in their lifetime. It has been labelled the 'common cold of psychology', giving an indication of how widespread the condition is. People experience a range of mental and physical symptoms (see page 52) characterised by feelings of frustration, sadness, lethargy and fear.

Depression in older people is relatively common and can be triggered by a number of factors that specifically relate to their age, and stage in life. But while it is natural to feel depressed after a distressing event like a bereavement, not every depressed person can point to an obvious cause. Some people experience a passage into depression that is sudden, severe, and has no apparent reason.

If the person you care for has already been diagnosed as depressed, or you suspect depression to be a problem but don't know how to take action, this book will give you a starting point for information. This chapter covers the topic in general. It looks at the range of problems that come under the umbrella term 'depression', at some of the reasons why the condition occurs, and at how it can affect people. A Fact Box gives some points that help put the illness into context. Later chapters look more fully at the characteristic medical symptoms of depression, the range of treatments available and your role as a carer.

A universal condition

Depression is a global phenomenon that has been recorded by many races throughout history, with documented evidence as long ago as the 5th and 4th centuries BC. Earlier sufferers may not have been given the kind of medical diagnosis that is available nowadays, but they have clearly described feelings that would sound familiar to modern doctors and psychiatrists.

Hippocrates (writing in around 420 BC)

'Fear or depression that is prolonged is melancholia.'

He goes on to describe symptoms such as 'an aversion to food, despondency, sleeplessness, irritability' and he noted that its cause lay in the 'individual's state of physical and psychological health'.

Fortunately for present day patients, much more is known about mental illness and the topic is less of a taboo subject. Modern psychiatry no longer considers depression to be a problem with the 'humours' – the view prevalent in the middle ages and focusing particularly on the increase in 'black bile in the autumn'. But the ancient diagnosis was not too far adrift (albeit using different reasoning) because, even today, depression is attributed to physical and biological causes. For example, the lessening of daylight hours (see page 7) is still a recognised cause.

Modern medical dictionaries describe depression as 'morbid sadness', 'dejection' and 'melancholy'. Such despairing terms illustrate deep gloom and indicate a far more worrying state of mind than the straightforward term 'unhappy'. Maybe it requires haunting words like 'melancholy', understood by generations of people, to help depict the kind of anguish that can dominate a depressed person's life, especially for the benefit of those who have no comprehension of how it feels to be depressed.

Mary

'When I'm depressed I feel like I'm in a dark place where the door is locked. I'm alone and I can't quite reach out to turn on the light or find a way out. I ask myself, how did I get trapped in here?'

3

Feeling 'blue'

Everyday 'blues' is a relatively common feeling, and many people with the blues might describe themselves as feeling 'depressed'. What they probably mean, however, is that their mood is low and they are not feeling very energetic. The body systems that control how we act and react are very complex, with 'mood' being one of the factors that help determine how well we cope with everyday situations. Our outward mood – be it sad or glad – is often indicative of what is happening emotionally deep inside and it usually affects how we deal with the world around us. If we are in a good mood we are likely to sail through the day but, if our mood state is low, we cope less well and small hitches feel like huge burdens. Everyday mood behaviour is probably linked to personality, making some people more prone to mood swings while others go through life on a much more even keel. However, it is important at this point to put this everyday feeling of 'the blues' into perspective. Feeling sad or glad is a normal response to life's events and, provided these feelings come and go and are relevant to the situation, they are quite harmless. The fact that someone feels upset after a difficult period is perfectly natural. It does *not* mean that person is suffering from the clinical illness, depression.

When a trained health professional talks to you about your relative's 'depression' they will not mean that your relative is suffering from mild blues. They are much more likely to be referring to a specific illness which has been medically diagnosed. Likewise, where the term is used throughout this book, it is referring to the illness not a transient low mood. It may be difficult at this stage for carers to understand the difference in meaning, but people who have experienced depression as an illness know that there is an enormous gulf between being depressed and simply feeling miserable for a short while. True depression is a debilitating illness, much more than merely feeling 'blue', and it doesn't disappear with a quick 'pick-me-up' remedy to lift the mood.

It is also important to understand that no-one chooses to suffer from depression; that people do not deliberately sink into a state where mental wretchedness rules their life. However hard it may be for carers to grasp this notion, they will find it easier to support (and protect) their relative if they can accept that it is not the person's fault, that their relative is not behaving in this manner just to 'get attention' or 'cause a bit of trouble'. It may be difficult to hold back sometimes from making a comment, but saying 'pull yourself together' or making accusations of 'self-pity' is not the straightforward solution it may appear. Your relative, after all, may be thinking 'if only life were that simple'! It is equally important to understand that the illness need not be a 'closed topic' which no one talks about. Carers and their older relatives should note that depressive disorder can be treated at all levels so, even if the symptoms seem mild, it is worth taking proper advice.

Who gets depression?

Depression can affect anyone at any age and certain factors have been identified that might make a person more prone to it:

- a family history of depression;
- losing a parent in childhood;
- physical or sexual abuse in childhood;
- long term debilitating illness.

Some people are more susceptible to depression, perhaps because of a genetic disposition. They might find their symptoms are more easily set off by other external events, such as:

- a period of stress;
- an unhappy event in their life;
- the development of a physical illness;
- long term use of certain medicines;
- lack of sufficient daylight.

Types of depression

Lesley (a general practitioner)

'Depression for any person is an individual experience. Their symptoms, the intensity, and especially the events that might have triggered the bout will be unique to them.'

Doctors, especially GPs, meet many people with depression – so they are used to recognising why people might need help. Traditionally, doctors have used the terms 'Reactive' and 'Endogenous' to describe depression. Although it is now thought these two categories have much more in common than used to be believed, the terms are still used by many GPs and may be found in books and leaflets. Whatever language your doctor uses, it is important you feel confident your concerns are being taken seriously.

Meta is a mental health worker

'If your GP tries to make light of your worries or he or she suggests that 'depression' is normal in older people, you can ask to speak to another doctor within the same practice for a second opinion.'

Reactive depression

This type of depression starts after an episode or life-period that has been particularly troubling. As the name suggests, the body systems (mental and physical) have been pushed a bit too far and a reaction occurs. The depressive period may start after an illness – influenza is a well known trigger – or following a distressing event such as a bereavement. For an older person the causative 'event' could be a move away from familiar surroundings into a care home.

Endogenous depression

The word 'endogenous' means 'coming from inside the body', so this type of depression is likely to be caused by some form of internal traumatic action, which may not always be easy to identify. This type of depression normally occurs because there is some kind of imbalance happening in the brain. The long term effects of pain, perhaps caused by severe arthritis, may be an example of an inner trigger. This form of depression is common and causes tiredness, sleep difficulties and feelings of self pity. The person may appear to grumble a lot about their aches and pains, and to believe (wrongly) that their low mood is a sign of old age and that nothing can be done to improve this.

Seasonal Affective Disorder (SAD)

SAD tends to occur as winter approaches because it is probably caused by a reduction in the length of daylight hours and a decrease in actual sunlight. It is associated with a disruption to the human body clock that rules our awareness of waking and sleeping hours (see 'circadian rhythms', page 12) and a seasonal variation in substances linked to body metabolism. Symptoms include the desire to sleep more and a hunger for sugary (carbohydrate) foods to help boost energy – which in turn can cause weight gain. It is also thought that symptoms are intensified in people living further north and under cloudier weather conditions. The arrival of spring can have quite a startling effect, generating a swift lift in mood. An estimated 80 per cent of SAD sufferers are female.

Postnatal depression

This form of depression is worth mentioning as many older women may remember experiencing the symptoms after childbirth. Because this type of depressive illness was less well known years ago, they may never have been officially diagnosed as suffering from a recognised condition. Postnatal depression lasts much longer than the milder form of 'baby blues' and the symptoms are more intense. 'Baby blues' involve mood swings and tearful spells, over a few days

7

only; the symptoms of true depression include sleep problems, enormous fears about coping adequately with a new baby and panic attacks. It affects between 10 and 20 per cent of mothers, starts a few weeks after delivery and comes on slowly. This results in many women, caught up in the tiring pattern of caring for a demanding baby, trying to ignore their own feelings of helplessness.

Manic depression

Doctors have classified depression into two types: a 'bipolar' type, which is characterised by bouts of manic and depressive episodes showing very obvious mood swings, and a 'unipolar' type where manic episodes do not occur. In their manic phases, a person with bipolar depression will exhibit a high level of exhilaration, over optimism and excessive energy. In their low phases, they sink into moods of absolute despair, with marked inactivity. It is most likely that people with this form of depressive illness will have been diagnosed in early adulthood. If an older person shows manic or very depressed behaviour, it is very likely they will have demonstrated these symptoms before. This type of bipolar depression is a completely different illness from the forms of depression discussed in this book and, therefore, is touched on only briefly.

Hypomania

Hypomania is a milder form of mania, which also occurs in manic depression or bipolar disorder. Its effects are less distressing and rarely impede day-to-day functioning to the point where hospital treatment is necessary.

Levels of depression

The types of depression described above can occur at varying levels – mild, moderate or severe – depending on the severity of the symptoms. The mildest form may cause little trouble with few symptoms. In moderate depression, the low feelings are more persistent and there may be noticeable physical symptoms. In severe depression, the patient feels very low most of the time and the associated symptoms are greater in number and intensity. This type of depression may give rise to strong psychological experiences where the person suffers from delusions and hallucinations. A depressed person may be suicidal at any level.

What causes depression?

Depression arises when a number of interacting factors, both biological and psychological, come together. There is no single cause and, like many illnesses, it is often difficult to distinguish between cause and effect. The brain is the organ that controls all our bodily functions – how we think, feel and behave – with the biological systems governing physical activity and mental and emotional states influenced by psychological processes. Doctors and researchers cannot fully explain the 'depression' phenomenon, and all the possible reasons put together make for a very complex picture.

The next two sections cover some of the factors that are associated with depression; although, as yet, there is no conclusive proof whether some of these factors are a *cause* or a *consequence* of depression. This information may help carers begin to understand some of the theory behind depressive illness. If you are not particularly interested in the biological and psychological influences on depression, you can skip over some of this theory and move on to the practical advice given in other chapters

Physical factors

Genes

There has been a great deal of research into the causes of depression, and scientists generally agree that people probably inherit genes that make them susceptible to developing depression. During the 19th century a German psychiatrist, Emil Kraepelin, found that heredity played a part in 80 per cent of the cases that came into his clinic in Munich. Present day figures, although lower, still make such a connection. Most studies show that the closer the blood ties, the greater the risk of becoming depressed. Fortunately, this connection within families is not a straightforward, direct-relationship link, because other effects such as environmental factors and family role modelling also play a part. It is not yet fully understood how genes are involved. But relatives should be comforted by knowing that while inheriting the gene may bring an *increased* risk, it does *not mean* that gene-carriers will automatically develop the disorder.

Neurotransmitters (brain chemicals)

Important research is taking place into the part played by neuro-transmitter action. The brain contains millions of nerve cells that communicate with each other via chemical elements, called 'neurotransmitters'. Messages are passed along from one nerve cell to the next by this neurotransmitter action. Their chemical names are *noradrenaline* and *serotonin* and it is possible that certain symptoms arise because one or both of these substances becomes under-active. The system is extremely complex with each nerve cell receiving and transmitting electrical information to thousands of other cells. These particular chemicals help to regulate some functions linked to depression, such as sleep patterns, appetite, sexual interest, and possibly mood. Antidepressant drugs help to normalise the function of these brain chemicals. There is still much to be learned about the working of the relevant chemical processes, the effects of drugs and the interaction between different parts of the nervous system.

Hormones

Another form of 'chemical messenger' which have been linked to depression, hormones are substances made and secreted by glands in the body in order to trigger other organs into action. Bouts of depression have been found to be more common in people during phases where hormone activity is increased, such as at the time of puberty or the menopause. They are also more common if hormonal activity is abnormal for some reason. One example of a hormonal disorder commonly associated with depression is myxoedema, a disease resulting from a deficiency in the hormone produced by the thyroid gland. Another example is Cushing's syndrome, a hormonal disorder where patients frequently suffer depression. A symptom of this disorder is the over-production of cortisol, a substance made by the adrenal glands, found near the kidneys. One study has found that levels of cortisol are increased in over 50 per cent of people with significant depression.

Water and electrolytes

As we have already seen, the effects of chemical changes in the brain probably play a major role in causing or exacerbating episodes of depression. Another contributing factor may be the part played by electrolytes which maintain the correct balance between different elements in the body tissues and fluids. Electrolytes are compounds which, when dissolved in water, change into electrically charged particles (ions) that can conduct electricity. An imbalance in the brain may interfere with the electrical charges transmitted between the brain cells. The amount of residual sodium (an electrolyte) has been found to be increased in patients with depression and mania. Further, changes have been reported in the movement of sodium and potassium (another electrolyte) in and out of cells during the recovery period following these illnesses.

Sleep patterns

The EEG (electo-encephalogram) patterns (see page 30) of non-depressed adults show that sleep patterns go through different stages, with a change in wave-forms at each specific stage. For example, deepest sleep normally occurs early in the night within the first two hours, and this stage is characterised by large wave-forms. Subsequent stages are characterised by a phenomenon known as rapid-eye movement (REM) – the time when we dream and our eyes move around rapidly. The first REM period should occur naturally about 90 minutes after we fall asleep and last for about five to ten minutes. It then recurs at regular intervals throughout the night and lasts longer towards morning. People suffering from depression have been found to begin this period earlier in the night (after about 25–60 minutes) and to experience periods of REM sleep more often than other people. At the same time, depressed people report having more frequent dreams, more unpleasant dreams and lighter sleep. Also, when they wake up they feel less refreshed than people who are not depressed.

Of course, lack of sleep in any person can lead to anxiety, irritability and hallucinations, whether the person is depressed or not. Fortunately, these physical problems abate either when the sleep pattern is restored or when the depression is lifting.

Body (circadian) rhythms

The biological rhythms that influence our daily patterns are closely linked to the environment in which we live. For example, one of the main interactions with nature (for humans and animals) is the light-dark, sleep-wake cycle. It is known that many body functions governing hormone output, temperature control and appetite work on an approximate 24-hour cycle. These cycles are commonly referred to as 'circadian rhythms'. Research has shown also that without external triggers (light-dark) the natural circadian rhythms in humans are slightly longer than 24 hours. Our systems would prefer to work more slowly but are speeded up by the influence of daylight. Sunshine hours play a very important role, providing a vital level of natural brightness that ordinary artificial light does not reproduce.

In a depressed person, various circadian rhythms may be involved. Sleep patterns are disturbed with early morning waking a common feature. Mood changes occur, with noticeable improvement as the day progresses ('diurnal variation'), and the production of cortisol (see page 11), normally at its highest during the night, does not reduce throughout the day to the low levels seen in a non-depressed person.

Physical illnesses

A number of physical symptoms – loss of weight, feeling debilitated, inability to sleep and general malaise – are indicative of poor health in general and are also linked to depression. Some illnesses are accompanied by early depression and, understandably, many people with depression often begin by believing that they are physically ill. In other ailments, such as chronic back pain or rheumatoid arthritis, depression may have developed because of the debilitating consequences of a long term illness. However, as we have found already with depression, the situation is rarely clear cut. The long term use of certain drugs (see below) may also further complicate the picture. It would be wise, therefore, for any person who is showing new and suspect depressive symptoms to consult a doctor to receive a proper check.

Medication

Taking certain groups of medicines for long periods is known to trigger depression, particularly in people who are prone to the disorder. Research into a specific drug treatment for high blood pressure, after patients taking it became depressed, led to connections being made with faulty neurotransmitter action. Other links are known to exist between steroid drugs used in the treatment of inflammatory conditions, chemotherapy drugs used in the treatment of cancer, and some drugs taken for the treatment of Parkinson's disease.

Psychological factors

Giving an exact description of the role played by the psyche or mind in depressive illness, is less easy than describing the part played by physical factors. While psychological influences do not cause depression by themselves, they will certainly influence the way in which a person responds to external situations and therefore how they respond to the symptoms and distress that are

13

encountered. So, psychological factors can increase vulnerability to depression; play a part in sustaining the disorder and affect how a depressed person views their illness.

Past history

A recurrent history of depression makes sufferers fearful that the illness will return, and their fears are likely to be magnified according to the severity of the depression they have already experienced. This type of emotion is understandable and not at all uncommon. However, that doesn't mean that the fear of recurrence has to dominate everyone's thinking. Take a pragmatic approach that recognises, on the one hand, that the illness might return, balanced against the optimistic viewpoint that a long, depression-free period is to be relished. When a depressive episode is over, tell yourself and your relative that for the time being it is 'past history' and that frequent referral to how bad they felt merely keeps the memory alive. Encourage a positive attitude. Life is to be enjoyed and no-one is betraying any trusts if they relax and anticipate an agreeable future. Part of living without depression is learning to live with the real possibility of it recurring.

Dealing with problems

People deal with problems in different ways, often related to the way they have tackled difficulties in the past and how well they have learned from their behaviour. A poor track record in coping with depression may cause people to try to ignore early symptoms and fail to seek treatment until the illness has become more serious. If family members pick up on signals that their relative is slipping into depression, it is worth asking themselves (and their relative) a few questions:

- How did we/they deal with this situation before?
- What lessons did we/they learn?
- What is new this time round?
- How much support did the family give/they need before?
- What are our joint/separate strengths?
- Will the depression go away if no one intervenes?

Judy is a community psychiatric nurse (CPN)

'Many families have a 'care plan' (action plan) already prepared and agreed, during a period of good health, which outlines how the person wants or does not want to be treated when they are ill, and which may cover such issues as hospital admission, medication etc. When drawing up such a plan it would be sensible to involve a CPN and your relative's GP to ensure that the actions specified meet with their approval and are within the law.'

Your ability to cope, individually and as a family, will depend greatly on the resources you have to hand. There are many coping strategies you can use, and a number of these are described in later chapters. If your relative's depression is recurrent, some of these may already be familiar to you. Others might offer new ideas for you all to try.

Thinking patterns

Nadia who has suffered from depression

'He praised events that went right and reminded me that there was another way of feeling – he gave me hope by being positive when I couldn't be.'

Many clinical psychologists believe that the way people think about themselves and the world generally will affect their behaviour, that is to say some people tend to be more negative than others in their approach to life. They might interpret experiences in a negative way and be extremely self-critical. They are likely to suffer from low self esteem, to blame themselves unduly for things that go wrong and look towards the future with fear and foreboding. The pessimistic person is the one who describes their cup as 'half empty' rather than 'half full'. The followers of this argument suggest that depressed thinking leads to depressed feelings. The opposite school of thought says that it is the other way around – depressed feelings are what trigger depressed thoughts. In other words the depression is the thing that comes first (for whatever reason) and this causes the development of negative ideas and opinions.

Other examples suggest that people who are depressed tend to be biased in their thinking and that this bias is likely to err towards the negative end of the scale. The following list illustrates ways in which this negative disposition might be demonstrated:

- Over exaggeration of how bad a situation was. If an activity didn't go quite as planned the tale they tell is full of woe, and they might resolve never to try that again. This type of person enlarges their faults and puts down their own good qualities
- Over generalising that, once a difficulty has occurred, things will always happen in that way again.
- Over personalising a problem by taking sole responsibility for failure. 'It's my fault' is an expression commonly used.
- Having a set of 'hard and fast' rules or engaging in 'inflexible thinking'. For example, saying that something is either right or wrong, or people are good or bad, without room for a middle road of thought.
- Jumping to negative conclusions even though the evidence is weak, or there are no obvious signs that support their view.
- Falsely weighting the balance between positive and negative aspects of a situation by playing down the good points and emphasising the bad. Sometimes this behaviour is taken to the level where a reversal takes place in their mind. For example, a pleasant or complimentary remark is turned into an insult by the belief that the giver of the compliment made it merely to hide a less pleasant aspect of the recipient's appearance.
- Setting impossible rules for achievement and the way they lead their lives – and often expecting others to act similarly. For example, insistence upon 'never being late' or setting high moral standards for truth telling, can lead to huge feelings of guilt or shame when these expectations become impossible to live up to, either for themselves or their friends and colleagues.

The examples above are not intended to outline 'right' or 'wrong' behaviour, and it is unlikely that a person with a depressive inclination would exhibit every one of the traits. However, families may notice a pattern developing, or their relative may be displaying increasingly worrying preoccupations or behaviour. If you feel concerned it will do no harm for them to consult their doctor for a check up (if they can be persuaded to). This type of negative behaviour can be treated well with a form of cognitive therapy described in Chapter 2.

When life is threatened

Unfortunately, the death toll from depression is sufficiently high to cause concern. The number of suicides in England and Wales is approximately 5,000 per year (*Understanding Depression*, Family Doctor Series/British Medical Association), of which about 3,000 deaths are the result of depression. About one per cent of deaths each year in England and Wales are due to suicide and the rate rises with age, being highest for women in their sixties and for men in their seventies. In addition to actual death many more depressed people will show suicidal behaviour such as storing tablets or writing suggestive notes. The threat of suicide is covered more fully in Chapter 3.

Agnes (whose mother took an overdose)

'However distressing it may be to confront the fact, you will be better equipped to deal with veiled threats, or take the necessary emergency action, if you and other family members have discussed how you might deal with a suicide attempt, as happened to my mother. If you feel that your relative's depression is getting worse, that they are talking about self-harm or not wanting to live, you must take these threats very seriously. I suggest that you speak to their doctor and take professional advice about how to proceed. If your relative expresses opinions about being a nuisance or out-

17

living their welcome, it is vital that – as family members – you show obvious signs of affection to make them feel wanted.'

Attitudes to depression

When a person is suffering from a common illness, everyone is usually anxious to know more about the condition – what might have caused it and how to put it right. Unfortunately, when depression is mentioned people frequently draw back rather than ask questions, because they are less sure how to respond. Many emotions are brought into play, not least the difficulty of explaining this illness to family members, friends and acquaintances – and having to deal with their reactions. Over the years, society at large has conveniently tucked mental health problems away into an area labelled 'not for everyday discussion', treating them in much the same way as cancer was treated 20 or more years ago. If people have no direct experience of depression, they may be ignorant, unsympathetic and intolerant.

Agnes

'I found it less stigmatising to focus on the causes that had contributed towards my mother's depression rather than discuss her physical and psychological symptoms. It was easier to rationalise the changes in her behaviour.'

Certain myths are still too common. One of the ways family members can support their relative is to shield them from some of these unhelpful attitudes. Look at the Fact Box below for ideas to help you combat some of the misconceptions you may meet. The most common fables are these:

- depression is a mild problem;
- depression is a passing mood that will soon change;
- depression is a weakness of mind over matter;
- depression is not life threatening like heart disease or cancer so there is no need to worry;
- depression cannot be treated.

Fact Box

- Poor mental health is one of the major public health problems affecting society today. Aside from stress (which is often self diagnosed) depression is the most common of all psychiatric illnesses affecting between three and four million people in the UK at any one time.

- At least one in five adults will suffer from depression. On average, each GP in the UK sees one patient with depression a day (BMA Family Doctor Series: *Understanding Depression*).

- Depression affects both sexes, but not equally. Figures suggest women will be affected significantly more than men in their lifetime, perhaps even twice as often. (BMA Family Doctor Series: *Understanding Depression*).

- Depression affects people in all walks of life, with a high proportion of sufferers failing to seek proper treatment. Famous sufferers include Queen Victoria, Sir Winston Churchill and a significant number of comedians including John Cleese and Tony Hancock.

- Industry, commerce, and the workplace generally lose several billion pounds each year because of depression – which leads to a loss of approximately 80 million working days.

- Depression threatens the quality of life (and life itself) for people suffering severe forms of other illnesses. It is linked to stroke and Parkinson's disease. A high proportion of the people who die from the affects of alcohol abuse also suffer from depression.

- Depression is treatable, with a range of effective drugs and physical and psychological therapies.

For more *i*nformation

ℹ️ *Understanding Depression*, Dr Kwame McKenzie, *Family Doctor Series* (available through most high street chemist shops)

ℹ️ Depression Alliance leaflet *'Everything You Need to Know about Depression'* (See page 207 for address).

Conclusion

This chapter has served as an introduction to depression. For some carers, if this is the first time your relative has suffered from the illness, it may be your first attempt at finding out more about a mental health problem; for other carers, whose relative has had recurring bouts of depression, reading this book may be an attempt to learn something new – about the illness or about how best to offer support.

The book has been written especially for carers and the information, advice and guidance is directed at their way of thinking. If you think it might also help your relative to understand their illness better, then share the book with them or read out parts that you feel are applicable. If the information helps with their recovery it doesn't matter who the book is aimed at!

The next chapter will tell you more about how depression is diagnosed and treated, and who provides professional care.

2 An introduction to diagnosis and treatments

It will not be easy to decide when the time has come to start doing something about the signs of depression in another person. But if the symptoms you are witnessing are enough to make you concerned, then it is time to take some action. Unless they know themselves very well, it is unlikely your relative will take the first steps. People who have not suffered from depression in the past may not recognise the significance of such unpleasant symptoms. Their decline may have been so gradual that they will be unaware of how bad things have become. Other people may think it is normal for your relative to feel depressed, especially if they have been through a distressing experience such as leaving a cherished home. There may be a widespread belief that 'there is nothing to be done'. Some people with depression may be determined to cope but do not realise that they are failing to do so, and the effort of trying to hide their feelings may increase their torment.

Depression affects significantly more women than men. The peak time for its appearance in women is 35–55 years, whereas men are more likely to be affected ten years later. Several million people receive treatment each year but, as many more remain undiagnosed, it is difficult to be sure of accurate figures. Estimates suggest that one in four women, and one in seven men, will suffer at some time during their lives. A research poll has shown that 78 per cent of the public believe (wrongly) that anti-depressants are addictive and about a third of the people questioned thought that they did not work. This level of understanding may be one of the reasons why people – especially older people – fail to seek medical treatment. They believe, mistakenly, that nothing can help.

Before you start reading this chapter, a note of caution should be sounded. Although it is beneficial to read about the methods used to recognise, diagnose and treat depression (in order better to understand the illness), trying to diagnose another person, or attempting self-diagnosis, are absolutely NOT recommended. If you suspect that your relative is suffering from depression, you should always seek (or encourage them to seek) advice from a professional person.

Recognising depression

Before looking at the symptoms of depression, it may be helpful to recap on some of the reasons why people become depressed. Traditionally, doctors have described depression as being 'endogenous', literally meaning 'coming from within', or 'reactive', meaning it has been set off by an identifiable life event. Although it is thought that endogenous depression has no obvious external cause, in reality it is often difficult to distinguish between the types so precise terms have become less important. Manic depression is a separate illness from the type of depression discussed in this book. While Chapter 1 outlined the range of physical and psychological theories believed to underpin the causes of depression, some potential trigger factors (such as hormones, sleep patterns and electrolyte disturbances) have not yet been shown conclusively to be either a cause or a consequence of the illness. Doctors do believe that depression is rarely spontaneous. So if a person has an inherent (genetic) tendency to develop depression, it is likely that the condition will be aggravated by an external trigger.

External life events which might set off a bout of depression include:

- loss, for example, loss of role, divorce, bereavement;
- money problems and debt;
- loneliness;
- poor housing conditions;
- family worries;
- work related pressures such as unemployment, redundancy or over-working.

A closer look at the events listed above reveals a pattern in which every situation involves some form of loss to the individual. Perhaps a spouse dies, or an older person is forced to leave their home, or a change occurs in an accustomed style of living. Ageing also brings the loss of youth, so closely associated in our society with vitality, mobility and physical attractiveness. Much loved children grow up and move away. Loss, for whatever reason, can cause people to feel negative about themselves. This can lead, in turn, to feelings of guilt, disappointment and lack of self-confidence, all forerunners to an episode of depression. In addition to mental and emotional upheaval, physical ill health and lowered resistance may also play a part. There are some obvious questions:

- What has set the depression going?
- Is this the person's first experience of the illness?
- Is it the return of a familiar illness?

Whatever the situation, the triggering factors will clearly be unique to your relative, so it shouldn't be too difficult to review the recent past and come up with some answers.

Lesley, a general practitioner

'Watching your relative and reporting to their doctor isn't "spying" on them because an accurate picture of their day-to-day actions will help me and other doctors to make an informed diagnosis. We rely on relatives who are in close contact to help us if they can.'

Before you take steps to intervene, think about the clues that 'set the alarm bell ringing' and keep some notes for a short while about how your relative is behaving. You can record your observations in two ways: the things your relative complains about (symptoms), and what you and other family members notice (signs). This information will be very useful in helping the doctor identify the best means of helping your relative back to health. The signals should be obvious if you know the person well. For example:

■ Has their relationship with people around them altered?

■ Are they complaining more than usual, however vaguely?

■ Is their work output suffering (at their formal workplace if they are still in paid employment or jobs about the home)?

■ Do they have difficulty concentrating?

■ Are they more irritable than usual, or more difficult to satisfy?

■ Have you noticed signs of poor body hygiene?

■ Do they complain of feeling lonely or neglected?

■ Have they become isolated and withdrawn?

■ Has their interest in leisure activities (such as hobbies, reading or watching TV programmes) dropped off?

■ Does the depression seem worse at particular times of the day, such as the mornings?

■ Have they started drinking (more) alcohol?

■ Have they become erratic in taking their medicines (either deliberately or through absent-mindedness)?

■ Do they say or do things which suggest they no longer care about what happens to them?

■ Are they talking about life not being worth living?

■ Are they showing signs of delusions – for example, becoming over guilty about past life events and wondering if their symptoms are a punishment from God?

There is no hard and fast rule about when to seek help. If the signs that you have observed are numerous then the time has come for you to be open with your relative. Read the clinical symptoms of depression listed below and compare the list with your notes. Unfortunately, there is no fail-safe approach that you can take if your relative does not wish to discuss their feelings or take medical advice. However frustrating it may be, try not to nag them into action. Older people can be very resistant to pressure, especially if they are fearful of what the doctor might diagnose. Tell them gently that you are concerned about their health and that you will give as much support as is necessary.

> ### *The Depression Alliance, a mental health charity*
>
> 'If people experience four or more symptoms, for most of the day, nearly every day, for over two weeks, they should talk to their doctor.'

The clinical symptoms of depression

The indicators that you have already observed might include several from the following lists, which are typical of the symptoms a doctor will ask about.

Mental/emotional aspects of depression

These include some of the following:

- persistent feelings of sadness and despair;
- loss of enjoyment in life;
- feelings of helplessness and hopelessness;
- difficulty in concentrating and indecisive behaviour;
- undue feelings of guilt and failure;
- chronic anxiety with accompanying feelings of panic and some form of compulsive behaviour;
- fears about the future – especially relating to their health;
- feeling that life is meaningless (which can lead to suicidal tendencies, even in mild depression).

Physical aspects of depression

The sort of physical problems that may appear include:

- disturbed sleep, particularly getting off to sleep or waking early in the morning;

■ poor memory;
■ difficulty in functioning in everyday activities;
■ tiredness and lethargy;
■ loss of appetite leading to other dietary problems such as weight loss and constipation;
■ over-eating with weight gain;
■ empty, emotionless facial expression;
■ becoming tearful more often than usual, or for no apparent reason;
■ self-harming behaviour;
■ a slowing down in movements, speech, thinking and response rates;
■ dislike of bright lights and loud noises;
■ lowered sexual drive and sexual problems.

Depression or just sadness?

Is your relative merely sad, or suffering from a depressive illness? It may not always be easy to determine this, especially if you have had no previous experience of this type of illness. You might tend to interpret the problem as 'sadness' for a number of reasons: because you are unsure about the difference; because you think you understand what it means to be sad but have no real insight into how a depressed person feels; because you might perhaps be unaware that depression can be treated.

Although depression can sometimes be triggered by a period of sadness (for example after a bereavement, see Chapter 3) it cannot be overstated that being sad and suffering from depression are totally different states of mind. Far from being linked, there are many distinctions between them. If you are unsure take another look at the list above. If the indications of depression are present, then help your relative to get a proper diagnosis.

The Depression Alliance

'Some people, especially older people, when they understand the significance of their symptoms, feel relief when labelled with an illness, even if it is a mental health one. Lots of clients have told us that they knew they just couldn't pull themselves together and were relieved when they realised that depression was an illness. Some of our older clients were also relieved that they did not have Alzheimer's disease or something similar.'

Anxiety and depression

It is recognised that anxiety and depression are linked. Their characteristics are very similar, and it is quite possible for a person who is over-anxious to be depressed at the same time. It works a bit like this: the feelings of anxiety cause the person to feel depressed and the depression creates feelings of fear, a typical sign of anxiety. The symptoms might occur simultaneously so it may be hard to tell them apart or to be sure which state came first. It doesn't really matter, as both conditions can be treated and medication for one can be taken at the same time as medication for the other. The lists below offer some clues, but there are differences and either state can exist separately, so it must be left to a professional person to make a proper assessment of your relative's mental state.

Similarities

The following may be experienced by people who are *either* depressed *or* anxious, as well as by many who are suffering from both conditions at the same time:

- fear of illness;
- fatigue;
- eating problems;
- sleep problems;
- poor concentration;

27

■ headaches and other pains;
■ panic attacks.

Differences

There are also some important differences between depression and anxiety. For example:

■ anxious people feel very emotional while depressed people can feel empty of emotions;
■ the thought processes in anxious people often speed up, leading to feelings of panic, while in depressed people this function slows down;
■ anxiety causes tension, quick jerky movements and stiff muscles; depressed bodies are often slumped and droopy with limp movements;
■ anxious people get diarrhoea caused by a speeding up of bowel movements and the reverse occurs in depression;
■ anxious people tend to seek external causes for their problems, while depressed people are more inclined towards self-blame, feelings of guilt and unworthiness;
■ anxious people have deep concerns about the future, but life never seems quite as hopeless as it does to people who are suffering from depression;
■ anxious people are fearful of death but do not wish to die; more seriously, depressed people frequently say they want to die and may have suicidal thoughts.

In one aspect in particular, people who are depressed and those who are anxious behave in a very similar fashion, even if the circumstances are different. People in each group show a strong inclination to re-live the past and re-enact unpleasant scenes over and over again in their mind. For example, anxious people who might have had panic attacks are fearful of repeating the distressing event so they worry about getting into situations in the future similar to those they believe to have triggered previous attacks; people who are depressed tend to dwell morbidly on any upsetting incident that has happened either to themselves or to their loved ones.

Diagnosing depression

Making a diagnosis of depression is not as straightforward as identifying an acute physical illness because the standard clues that doctors use (such as raised temperature, severe pain or vomiting) are absent. When assessing any mental illness, doctors will ask for in-depth detail before making their diagnosis and deciding on suitable treatment. Much of the investigation will centre round information you and your relative provide, so the doctor will spend time questioning you about what you have observed, and your relative about how they feel. This might include giving details of any personal and family history and/or lifestyle factors that might have a bearing on the diagnosis. At the same appointment, the doctor will probably do a physical examination as it is important to rule out other diseases for which depression is also a symptom.

Lesley, a general practitioner

'The overall signs, symptoms and history both help me to get a complete picture and give a baseline against which future progress can be monitored.'

Additional tests

The doctor might decide that a number of checks are required. These include blood tests, which will be done by the GP, as well as other tests which will only be ordered after referral to a specialist. The specialist will explain at the time why each one is necessary.

- **Blood tests** find out whether various organs are functioning normally. Examples include thyroid function tests, liver function tests, blood glucose levels.
- **Computed tomography (CT) scans** look at the any underlying degenerative changes to the brain or vascular (blood) system using specialist x-ray techniques.

29

- **Electo-encephalograms (EEG)** take a reading of brain patterns using a harmless test where electrodes are attached to the scalp to measure electrical wave activity in the brain. These wave patterns are normal in depression but show signs of change in degenerative brain disorders.
- **Psychological tests** measure any cognitive impairment (alertness). Depressed patients manage this type of test well but a person with dementia would show evidence of reduced function.

Be sure that your relative is clear about the next stages, especially if decisions have to be made about treatment. You can help by listening carefully on their behalf and taking notes if this would help you remember words and instructions. Later, in a quieter moment, you can both recall what you heard and help each other to remember what information was given. Try not to feel rushed. It is probable that your relative will be referred to a specialist if their symptoms are severe.

Measuring depression

A professional person might assess your relative using a scale or measurement that is commonly recognised by other people trained in the field of mental health. One such scale is the *Beck Depression Inventory* (BDI) which asks patients to complete a questionnaire that offers them a multiple choice of answers in each section. The person is asked to circle the appropriate answer that best describes how they have felt in the previous week. The scores are then added up in a similar way to lifestyle questionnaires that appear in magazines. As depression cannot be measured objectively, any such level will necessarily be subjective. However, the setting of a baseline score gives a position that everyone can refer to later. Doctors in different parts of the country – or with different professional interests – may use varying methods to help assess levels of depression.

Note It is not wise to try to diagnose another person or to undergo self diagnosis without proper professional guidance.

Agnes

'At home my mother and I came up with a personal rating that acted as a guide to her level of depression on a day to day basis, alongside any treatment or self-help measures that had been recommended by a professional person. We scored the rating on a scale of one to ten. Point 1 (not at all depressed) at the lower end of the scale related to her mood when life was good and happy; in contrast, she used Point 10 (full of despair) at the upper end of the scale to mark the times when she was very low. This scale was a helpful indicator to give me a snapshot into her mood, especially when she didn't want to talk much.'

Treating depression

Who treats mental illness?

This section opens by introducing the people you and your relative might meet in the course of their encounter with depression, then goes on to look at when and how you might come across them. The main professional people working to diagnose and treat any form of mental illness are:

- **General practitioner (GP)**: a community doctor based at the local health centre or surgery. The GP is the key figure whom your relative should visit first and, depending on the severity of the illness, they will be able to deal with most aspects of the illness – from diagnosis to treatment. All treatment given by the GP is arranged through the local surgery.
- **Psychiatrist**: a medically trained doctor who specialises in the treatment of emotional and mental disorders. Psychiatrists are based at district or psychiatric hospitals and they can usually see patients at home or an outpatients' clinic. The GP will make the appointment for your relative. Patients are only referred to a psychiatrist if their depression is severe or perhaps not responding well to treatment. The majority of older people with a reactive form of depression are unlikely to need

31

to see a psychiatrist, and even less likely to require a stay in hospital. Occasionally, day care provision is offered at a specialist centre.

- **Mental health (or psychiatric) nurse**: a trained nurse who specialises in caring for people with mental illness. Mental health nurses work in hospital and community settings, the latter based at a GP surgery, community hospital or health centre. Your relative is most likely to be visited at home by a community psychiatric nurse (CPN) who will work closely with the GP (as well as with the psychiatrist, if one is involved) as part of a community team.

- **Psycho-geriatrician**: a psychiatrist who concentrates on working with older people with mental health problems. This role is usually hospital-based; however, the specialist will work closely with the community-based team treating your relative. Nowadays most health districts provide this type of specialised, 'expert' care.

- **Clinical psychologist**: a professionally trained person who deals with the mind and its method of working. Many psychologists carry the title of 'Dr'; however, it is most likely that this refers to a scientific degree rather than a medical qualification.

- **Psychotherapist**: a professional person who is trained to treat patients with therapies that relate to their mind. All illnesses, even physical disorders have some effect on the mind, eg learning how to deal with pain. In the case of depression, the psychological effects of the illness tend to dominate.

- **Counsellor**: a therapist who is trained to listen to someone in an unbiased way and help them make decisions and take practical steps towards recovery.

Appointments with professional people

The first interview with any of the people listed above is likely to be similar and you, as the main carer, can remain in the room as long as your relative feels comfortable about your presence. If they are not able to speak well for themselves, their GP will most probably suggest that you are present. At the first appointment the GP will ask about the recent events and symptoms that have led you to come along for advice. This will take a short while. The GP may then ask you both to return for a subsequent and perhaps longer appointment. Interviews with other professional people, who may not know your relative, usually take longer as they will ask a series of questions to find out more about them as a person. It is natural to feel apprehensive, but doctors and nurses will try to put you at ease and the sort of questions that are likely to be asked will explore obvious points rather than be deeply searching.

In preparation for the appointment, it may help if you write an account of how things have been. Short notes will do and you can refer to these at the meeting if you feel nervous. Always mention the most important problem or symptoms first rather than coming to the crux of the matter from an oblique angle. Your relative can expect to be asked about:

- their personal background;
- their medical history;
- their current situation;
- the way the depression has developed;
- how it is affecting their day to day living;
- whether they have felt depressed in the past, and if so;
- whether they received treatments and what the effects of such treatments were.

If you see people other than the GP you may feel that you and your relative have said it all before. This is probably true, and notes will have been recorded each time. Be patient as individual people like to ask questions in their own style and, most importantly, they will want to hear your personal version in your own words rather than relying solely on the written information supplied by the GP. Talking to you both at length is one of the ways they can get to know you better so they can make decisions about the best methods of treatment.

Treatment methods

It is very important to understand and accept that this period of depression may be a normal reaction to a recent life-event. It is *not* a sign that your relative is becoming senile, nor does it mean that they are 'going mad'. Unfortunately, neither does it mean that your relative will definitely not develop dementia in the future as some types of dementia are caused by vascular problems ('mini-strokes'). Depression Alliance advise families to reassure their relatives that depression is not connected, nor does it lead to, senile dementia. In fact, the feelings of depression at this moment in time may be the body's way of dealing with something that has made the person deeply unhappy. However, if it is apparent that the cloud is not lifting and they are finding it increasingly difficult to cope, their doctor will suggest the time has come to use more focused treatments.

As the section above indicates, most people with depression are treated by their family doctor and the treatment takes two main clinical forms – 'talking therapies' and 'medication'. In addition, family and friends can provide support and encourage various 'self-help' methods to complement the recommended treatments.

The different approaches are often described in the following way: *talking* is about helping with feelings, and *medication* (or pills) is about relieving symptoms. A small number of patients who do not get better with these basic treatments are likely to be referred to a psychiatrist for more specialised care. In extremely severe cases the psychiatrist may advise a course of electrical treatment, known as ECT (electro-convulsive therapy). This type of treatment is used relatively rarely.

Talking therapies

It may sound vague but simply talking about feelings is a great help to many people. A trained therapist or counsellor will help your relative to explore, confront and hopefully come to terms with their depression. These talking sessions are spaced over weeks or months, progressing at a pace that suits the needs and health of the person. Your relative will not be rushed into a whirl-wind of treatment with which they cannot cope as therapists know that opening up recent or old emotional wounds takes time and emotional energy. The person has to be motivated to do this rather than be coerced. They may not be ready to start talking in depth while their depression is still at an acute stage.

Working with a therapist is beneficial for a number of reasons. Your relative may reveal or dredge up episodes in their life that have long been suppressed and here the therapist can exert more pressure that any family member would dare (or know how). Putting their thoughts into words helps people to sort out their feelings and a professional person is trained to probe a little deeper. The therapist will report back to other professionals if it is important that details of the case are shared. They are also able to offer your relative their sole attention for the duration of the session. This is a good morale booster in itself, as well as being something that few family members have the time to do. Hopefully, their troubles will begin to make sense and your relative will develop the confidence to move forward or accept that some situations cannot be altered.

One of the benefits of talking as a method of treatment is that it often works alone without the need to use anti-depressant drugs; if not it might take place alongside short term medication. There are two main ways in which your relative can talk to a professional person: counselling and psychotherapy. Both treatments are designed to look at what might be the cause(s) of the depression, as well as at what is happening right now that might be preventing the person from 'getting back to normal'. Therapists and counsellors are trained to offer support and guidance, particularly with patients whose confidence is low.

Counselling

Joseph, a counsellor

'Close family members should not feel guilty at this point that they should have done more to help. As therapists we understand that sometimes it is harder to talk about problems to a loved one than it is to unburden to an independent person. We are trained to listen and understand without passing opinion; this non-judgemental approach can bring enormous ease.'

Counselling is less formal than psychotherapy and takes a very practical approach to helping clients deal with their problems. The purpose of counselling is to help people focus on their main worries, so they can best solve those problems that can be tackled and move forward in their lives. The counsellor asks questions, listens to the responses and helps the person come to terms with any difficulties that cannot be resolved. If it becomes apparent that the depression is linked to other problems, the counsellor may recommend that your relative visits another agency that can provide very specialist counselling. For example, bereavement counsellors will help a client accept that the person for whom they are grieving will never return to their lives in a physical sense although it might not always be possible to achieve this understanding. Counsellors specialising in problems connected with relationships or alcohol will focus on those issues. Counselling is usually short term as the counsellor will know early on whether your relative is responding to their help and support.

Psychotherapy

Psychotherapists take a more formal approach in helping patients deal with the effects of their depression, using psychological procedures based on sound medical theories about how the mind works. The term 'psychotherapy' covers a broad range of methods each focusing on a different technique to achieve results. A therapist may use more than one method during the course of the treatment; the method to be used and the reasons why it has been chosen will be explained to your relative at each stage. Therapists encourage people to look into the origins of their problems and the discussions between therapist and patient are designed to help relieve emotional distress, and possibly change the way the person thinks about themselves and situations. For example, negative thinking may be influencing their behaviour and causing them to blame themselves for their depression – which in turn will cloud their judgement about other aspects of their life.

Therapists and counsellors work on a one-to-one basis initially. But they then might suggest that the person moves on to group sessions. If family relationships are involved other family members may be asked to take part. Psychotherapy sessions are usually spread over a longer period than basic counselling as people are rarely offered this type of therapy unless their problems are deep-seated. No one, including your relative, will be forced to participate in any form of counselling or therapy against their wishes. Like counselling, if the therapist believes the depression is connected with something specific (for example, a bereavement) a worker from another agency might become involved.

The limitations of talking treatments

Joseph, a counsellor

'Counsellors and psychotherapists work in similar ways. Neither person can cure your relative of depression at the wave of a magic wand, and it will help us if your relative is motivated to receive help.'

Before the counselling sessions start, you could help by gently encouraging your relative and asking a few questions to elicit whether or not this person:

- is ready to be helped;
- is prepared to work with the professional, and follow their guidance;
- understands that decisions about changes in behaviour lie with themselves;
- accepts that it may take a while to achieve results.

The counsellor or therapist is trained to:

- be sensitive in their approach;
- show respect for your relative's rights;
- be strictly impartial;
- advise your relative and their doctor if it seems that treatment is being attempted too soon, perhaps because emotions are too raw;
- discourage your relative from becoming over dependent on their support;

37

- work within the law (ie they will not condone any misuse of prescribed or illegal drugs, and will not support any attempts at suicidal action);
- respect any religious views your relative might hold;
- avoid intervening directly in practical matters such as financial difficulties or problems with accommodation.

Confidentiality

Melanie, a therapist

'The treatment is always a private and confidential affair between myself and a client. If they wish to talk to anyone about the sessions, that is their choice alone. As a family you must resist the temptation to pry, drop hints or contact the therapist direct, without your relative's permission.'

This may not be an easy message to hear, especially as you want to help. Try to be patient, bide your time and you will become involved when the time is right. This may be immediately or later on, when your relative has become more adjusted to the situation. If and when they do talk to you, it is still important to respect their privacy and not blurt out details to others without permission. It may be less stressful for your relative if you are the person who explains the situation to others on their behalf, but discuss this approach with your relative before making assumptions. The therapist would advise you how to do this if you are unsure about how far to reveal your relative's medical details. They would also tell you about self-help methods that you and your relative can practise between sessions or after the course of therapy is completed.

Safeguards

It is hoped and assumed that counsellors and therapists are properly trained and work to an ethical code of practice. Unfortunately, unscrupulous practitioners have sometimes exploited older and/or emotionally vulnerable patients in the past. If at any point you are worried it is quite appropriate for you to speak to your relative's doctor to allay your concerns. The relevant professional bodies keep records and often publish directories of the therapists and counsellors registered in the UK.

For more *i*nformation

i Counselling is available through the NHS or by private arrangement. Ask at your relative's GP practice, or the Community Psychiatric Nurse or The British Association for Counselling and Psychotherapy (see page 203) about locally-based counsellors.

i Patients are referred to an NHS psychotherapist by their GP or psychiatrist. Private therapy is available outside the NHS (although the therapist might also work within the NHS). Contact The British Association for Counselling and Psychotherapy (see page 203) for a list of registered psychotherapists.

i CRUSE – Bereavement Care offers information, counselling, support and encouragement to bereaved people (see page 207).

i Relate offers counselling to couples or individuals who are experience problems in their relationship (married or otherwise) given by professionally trained counsellors (see page 214).

i Alcohol Concern offers information about the problems and risks of alcohol abuse (see page 202).

Medication

The information given in this section is intended only as a brief outline of the main medicines used to treat depression and anxiety, so that you and your relative understand why medication is so important and what effects it can have. Always check the information given on the label and if you or your relative are unsure about any aspect of the medication they are taking, check with their own doctor or ask the pharmacist at the local chemists.

It can be confusing for a lay person but the words 'drug' and 'medicine' mean the same thing in medical terms. The collective name for the drugs (medication) used in the treatment of depression is 'antidepressants'. When, and if, your relative is offered medication will depend largely on the severity of their symptoms and the length of time they have been unwell. Antidepressants are highly effective at helping people regain their feeling of normality. They are not the same as tranquillisers, although people usually become less anxious while being treated. Antidepressants may be used to treat anxiety alongside depression or additional medication for anxiety may be prescribed at the same time. Antidepressant drugs are not addictive.

Depression Alliance

'Between 60 and 70 per cent of people who are treated with antidepressants will make a good recovery.'

A course of antidepressants is usually prescribed over many months and it is important to understand that it will not have an instant effect. All categories of drugs work in the body in different ways; for example, antibiotics start to kill bacteria immediately, but the action of antidepressants is much slower. Antidepressants work by normalising the activity levels in the brain of certain chemicals that influence mood, and a sufficient quantity of the drug needs to build up in the body before it begins to work effectively. There should be noticeable changes within 3-6 weeks, though this may be as long as 6–8 weeks in some patients, because antidepressants do not work very quickly in older people. Even so, your relative may sleep better and feel less tense from a very early stage. It is essential that your relative continues to take the tablets even when they are feeling much better. The recommended duration is at least six months depending on the time of year and severity of the initial illness.

Depression Alliance

'The chances of becoming depressed again are reduced significantly if an antidepressant is taken for six months after the first episode; for up to two years after a second relapse and for three to five years for recurrent depression.'

There is no need to feel concerned about taking medication for this length of time as the drugs are not addictive. However, even though patients do not become dependent on the drugs in an addictive sense, unpleasant symptoms such as headaches and nausea can occur if the drug is discontinued suddenly. These effects are due to the withdrawal of chemicals from the brain. The doctor will advise your relative about when and how to stop, and give them a regime that reduces the dosage gradually.

Harry is a general practitioner

'You could explain this non-addictive quality by telling your relative that people with addictions crave the next dose and need increasing levels of the drug to achieve the same effect – neither desire should be present with antidepressants.'

Side effects

Among other side effects which tend to occur, constipation and a dry mouth are common. You can help your relative deal with these symptoms by encouraging them to drink more, to eat snacks that keep their mouth fresh and foods which are high in fibre to help to reduce constipation (see pages 96–97). All drugs have side effects in some way because all drug treatments introduce a 'foreign' material into the body; fortunately, only a minority of people experience effects that are so severe they interfere with treatment. Look on side effects as a good sign that the medication is working. If your relative is feeling unwell, encourage the view that

41

short term discomfort is much easier to bear than the long term misery created by untreated depression. Different antidepressant tablets have different side effects so if one type is causing a problem the doctor can offer an alternative. Sometimes starting the doses slowly with a reduced dose for a few days helps to cut down on the nuisance. Research continues into producing more potent antidepressant drugs with lowered side effects.

Antidepressants vary as to what time of day they are taken, depending on the type of depression. If your relative still drives a car or is unsteady on their feet, be sure that they understand the potential consequences of feeling drowsy, for their own safety. The drowsy effect should wear off and it has its advantages in helping to induce sleepiness at night. Most tablets do not interfere with other medications such as antibiotics and pain killers, but it is unwise to drink alcohol as the combination will enhance drowsiness. Certain foods are definitely prohibited because they contain a substance called 'tyramine', a natural substance found in the body, which is also a component of the MAOI drugs (see page 43 for more details). An excessive level of tyramine can bring about a serious reaction, making the person feel hot or flushed or suffer a severe headache.

Harry, a general practitioner

'If you don't understand about any treatment ask – again and again if necessary.'

Drugs for depression

Although there may seem to be a range of antidepressants, in reality there are only a few main groups. Firstly, there are several variations of the same drug available which enables doctors to prescribe the best 'match' for the person's symptoms. It may take several attempts to find the drug which gives the best results with the fewest side effects. Secondly, different manufacturers give the same basic drug a different colour and trade name. Think of pills like cornflakes on a supermarket shelf – the names and the packaging may be different but the cereal looks the same!

There are currently about 30 different drugs licensed for use as antidepressants in the UK by pharmaceutical companies. Product licences are awarded only after strict clinical trials have been carried out to check the effectiveness and safety of the medication. There are some medical disorders where it may be unwise to take certain types of antidepressant drugs. All GPs should be aware of these contra-indications, but if a change occurs in your relative's health while they are taking antidepressants, do contact their doctor for advice.

The main groups used in the treatment of depression are:

- **Monoamine oxidase inhibitors (MAOIs)** While these drugs are not now being prescribed as often as they used to be, you may still come across them. They are used to regulate certain chemicals (noradrenaline and tyramine), important elements of brain metabolism. Examples include, isocarboxazid (trade name, Marplan) and phenelzine (trade name, Nardil).
- **Selective serotonin re-uptake inhibitors (SSRIs)** These are used in the control of nerve impulse transmission which in turn has an effect on mood swings. Citalopram (trade name, Cipramil) is regularly used in older people, as its benefits have been thoroughly studied in the treatment of members of this age group. Fluoxetine (trade name, Prozac) is another example of this group of drugs.
- **Serotonin and noradrenaline re-uptake inhibitors (SNRIs)** These drugs work in a different way to the group above but general information given by your relative's GP about SSRIs also applies to this group. An example of this group of drugs is venlafaxine (trade name Efexor).
- **Noradrenergic and specific serotonergic antidepressants (NaSSAs)** These drugs (for example, mirtazapine, trade name, Zispin) work by increasing the levels of both serotonin and noradrenaline in the brain.
- **Tricyclic Antidepressants (TCAs)** These also have an effect on the metabolism of the brain, this time by blocking the effect of neurotransmitters. They are especially useful in treating physical symptoms such as sleep problems and loss of appetite.

■ **Lithium** This is used to help control the mood swings found in manic depression.

Missed doses

The main advice for dealing with a missed dose is: Don't worry. Advise your relative to take their tablets as soon as they remember, provided it is only a few hours after the usual time. If it is longer, in order to keep the timing sequence correct, wait until the next dose is due and take the normal dose as usual – do not take a double amount to make up the difference. More guidance on the safe use of medicines is given in Chapter 3.

Drugs for anxiety

Tranquillisers, used to reduce anxiety, are not modern; however, the rapid increase in their consumption is relatively recent. Drug groups commonly prescribed in the early part of the last century, barbiturates for example, caused many problems. Then, new types of anti-anxiety drugs (trade names, Librium and Valium) entered the market. For many years these drugs seemed to be the answer as they were very effective and produced few side effects. Then the good news 'bubble' burst when it became clear that these drugs were causing apparent addiction and dependency. Doctors began to express concern as the figures for tranquilliser use continued to increase. During the years 1965–1970 the number of prescriptions supplied rose by 110 per cent (30 million prescriptions were written in Britain in 1970). Looking at the tranquilliser problem retrospectively studies have shown that many of these patients, predominately women, were often suffering from depression.

The rate of tranquilliser prescribing has fallen considerably since the period illustrated above. When used correctly they are beneficial in the treatment of mild depression as they reduce associated feelings of anxiety and are relatively safe to take as a form of medication. But tranquillisers lose their potency if taken long term, and they are not effective in dealing with depression as a sole form of treatment because their action does not affect mood disorders.

If your relative has been prescribed tranquillisers alone it is quite in order to ask their doctor to explain why.

For more *i*nformation

ⓘ Depression Alliance leaflet *'Depression and Antidepressants'* (address on page 207).

Electro-convulsive therapy (ECT)

Electro-convulsive therapy is given only when the symptoms of depression are causing severe distress and when the person concerned is failing to respond to other forms of treatment, or when they have another medical condition which makes taking antidepressant medication difficult or impossible. ECT involves passing a current of electricity through the brain, after the patient has been given a general anaesthetic and medication to relax their muscles. ECT has a negative image, partly due to its misuse in cinema films in the past; however, the actual shock lasts for a split second and the anaesthetic should prevent any pain being felt. The whole treatment takes about fifteen minutes and the patient is unconscious throughout the treatment.

Doctors are unsure why ECT works, but those who prescribe this treatment do so in the best interests of their patients because, for certain categories of people, ECT works well. It somehow raises their mood and has a quicker action than medication. There are several theories about which area it affects, covering neurotransmitters, hormone action in the brain and circadian rhythms but as yet no true answers. The course is spread over several weeks, with between six and twelve sessions given twice weekly. Unfortunately, ECT is not without side effects as many patients report a degree of confusion and memory loss, headaches and some muscle discomfort. Most side effects clear up very quickly and treatment is given under safe and well-controlled conditions.

Electro-convulsive therapy will not cure depression but it may be the type of treatment needed to raise the spirits of a severely depressed person. However, as drug therapies continue to improve ECT is recommended less frequently, but it remains an alternative treatment.

Light therapy

Light treatment (phototherapy) is used especially for those people whose depression is caused by seasonal variations in natural light (see Seasonal Affective Disorder, page 7). Medical research has shown that a significant number of patients (60–70 per cent) who suffer with winter depression are helped when using a light box. The therapy works in a very simple way and is quite safe. The improvement rate can be swift with changes noticeable after one to two days and the best results felt after about a week. The person sits in front of a special box that gives off light rays, many times brighter than traditional indoor light. The treatment can be done at any time of day and the best position is about one metre (three feet) from the light source. The special light rays are picked up through the eyes; yellow household-type light directed onto the skin does not work. Ideally, the treatment should last for a minimum of two hours with maximum effect after four hours. To achieve lasting results the therapy must be taken consistently or the person will quickly notice a relapse. The light rays are thought to affect the seasonal variations that occur naturally in two substances in the body: melatonin and serotonin. Melatonin is a hormone secreted by the brain (from the pineal gland). It is normally secreted only at night and is thought to induce sleep and helps to regulate waking/sleeping cycles. The release of melatonin into the bloodstream is affected by exposure to light, hence an application of bright light in the morning should inhibit further supplies being released. (Melatonin should not be confused with the similar-sounding *melanin*, the dark pigment found in the hair, the eye and the skin). Serotonin participates (amongst other functions) in the transmission of nerve impulses. It is also thought to play a part in mood variation. (See SSRI drug treatments page 43.)

Self-help

A belief in the philosophy of 'self-help' is very important for many people, as the idea that they are helping to take some personal control over their illness can give them the confidence to move forward. Self-help activities cover several different techniques many of which can be very worthwhile, especially when used together. By practising a combination of methods it may be possible to alleviate or prevent mild depression. Alternatively, the techniques can be used to complement the treatments prescribed by the doctor. Self-help practice should not be used as the sole approach, however, if your relative's depression is sufficiently severe to warrant professional clinical treatment. Self-help methods include:

- using gentle exercise as a pleasurable way of lowering anxiety and improving mood; however, it is important not to push your relative into activity before they feel ready, as many people with depression feel constantly tired;
- attending group sessions, perhaps run by a charity such as the Depression Alliance (where a trained group leader will help the members share experiences with each other and gain mutual benefit and support);
- practising complementary therapies such as aromatherapy or reflexology (fully described in Chapter 8);
- talking with family and friends;
- planning a variation in routine that brings pleasure and a change of scene – start in a small way with an easy outing such as tea with a friend, and lead on to something more adventurous like a weekend away;
- gathering information from mental health charities, the library and media articles;
- contacting a specialist helpline (again this type of support is most likely to be provided by a charity dealing with mental health or related problems);

- a change as simple as introducing a few novel additions to their basic diet may help your relative to look forward to the next meal. For hints about improving lifestyle, eating well and improving lifestyle, see Chapter 5.

For more *i*nformation

ℹ Self-help type support is offered by:

ℹ CRUSE – Bereavement Care (address on page 207).

ℹ Depression Alliance (address on page 207).

ℹ The Manic Depression Fellowship (address on page 212).

ℹ MIND (National Association for Mental Health), (address on page 212).

ℹ The Samaritans, (address on page 215).

ℹ SAD Association, (address on page 215).

ℹ Scottish Association for Mental Health (address on page 215).

Conclusion

This chapter has provided basic information to help you and your relative be more aware of the methods used to recognise, diagnose and treat depression. In many ways the process of understanding an illness can act as a resource in helping towards recovery because understanding something is a strong factor in our ability to cope with it. Hopefully, you will be heartened by the knowledge that a choice of treatments is available. You may also feel more confident that your relative's doctor will take their distress seriously and be relieved to discover that depression in older people is not uncommon. The thought of your relative being admitted to a psychiatric hospital might have been a real concern for you. However, this is unlikely unless their condition becomes very serious. Occasionally people with severe depression require the type of intensive care that is best given in a hospital environment, often because their life is felt to be at risk because of suicide attempts or poor nutrition. Chapter 4 gives more detailed advice on coping with the reality of severe depression, including a section on how to deal with threats of suicide and emergency action if an attempt is made to end life. The next chapter looks more closely at how depression affects older people.

3 Focus on depression in older people

As the previous chapters have indicated, the word 'depression' describes an illness that is much more serious than merely being sad. The overall manifestation of the illness includes both physical and mental symptoms, which rarely recede without treatment. People who are suffering true depression feel helpless and hopeless and, in addition to their mental distress, they have to live with sleeplessness, poor appetite, loss of energy and general aches and pains. All of this adds up to a very unpleasant experience.

Depression in an older person must never be viewed as 'normal', although the reasons that might exacerbate the illness are undoubtedly more common in this age group. Factors such as retirement, feelings about loss of status, physical discomfort and emotional upheavals can all happen in later years and some people, more prone to depression, are consequently more affected by these life events. Unfortunately, there is a widely held view in society that such characteristics as loss of motivation and zest for life, reduced spontaneity of action, melancholy and increased anxiety are the natural result of an ageing body. This is definitely a myth. In fact, these are clear signs of a depressive illness and, like most other mental or physical conditions, they respond well to treatment. Whatever the causes might be, it is important to remember that suffering from depression is not anyone's fault. The Royal College of

Psychiatrists states that people who have had depression are no more at risk of dementia than anyone else. Depression and dementia are usually completely separate conditions.

This chapter focuses on aspects of depression that are particularly relevant to older people.

How common is depression in later life?

It is probable that a mild form of depression is quite common in later life, as actual figures are almost impossible to predict. Depression is known to be one of the most under-diagnosed and under-treated medical disorders at any age, and the risk rate increases with age. Among the over 65 age group, the likelihood of developing depression is three times greater than among younger people. (Some studies have estimated that approximately 12–15 per cent of all people aged over 65 years suffer from depressive symptoms, which escalate with age). Among patients living in care and those admitted to hospital the rate is probably higher. However, figures do vary, possibly because surveys never ask identical questions and the purpose of each piece of research is usually different. So, despite the fundamental factors commonly found at this age, it must not be assumed that the majority of older people are depressed. The Royal College of Psychiatrists' figures are less discouraging: it suggests that, at any one time, fewer than one (older) person in six feels so depressed that they or others would notice; and fewer than one in 30 older people are so depressed that doctors would diagnose a 'depressive' illness.

What influences depression in older people?

The causes in this age group are very much the same as those out-lined in the previous chapters, and the symptoms are sufficiently debilitating to be a real problem. Unfortunately, many of the predisposing factors are more likely to occur as people get older, thus making the situation worse. People who are already susceptible to depression are more likely to succumb to the illness when prime factors are present. An episode of depression is rarely set off by a single cause. It is much more likely that several things have come together in your relative's life to make them more vulnerable. The list might include:

■ a distressing event such as divorce, the death of a spouse or close friend, the loss of a pet or a move into a care home;

■ the incidence of past depression, whether diagnosed and treated, or not;

■ the loss of physical health and ability (for example, a long term illnesses such as Parkinson's disease, rheumatoid arthritis, a sudden stroke and/or reduced sensory powers) or any other condition that seriously affects the quality of life;

■ the long term use of certain tablets frequently prescribed to older people – medication to reduce high blood pressure and steroid therapy being common examples;

■ physical symptoms similar to those found in depression which are also indicative of other illnesses common in old age but have remained undiagnosed (a hormone imbalance that reduces the activity of the thyroid gland (myxoedema) is one such example that tests would uncover if it were present).

Dealing with loss and loneliness, or with unpleasant and disabling symptoms, and the thought that such a state of affairs could persist for the rest of one's life, is sufficiently disturbing to make many people feel depressed.

What is different in older people?

The main differences between depression in younger and older people can be categorised under the following headings:

■ **Physical symptoms** Older people are more likely to draw attention to physical problems which they can easily describe – for example, headache pains, stomach upsets, fear of fatal illnesses, memory impairment, tiredness and insomnia.

- **Emotional symptoms** Older people are less likely to tell their doctor about changes in mood or reduced interest in life or loss of desire for social contact. If they describe their emotional feelings they might use terms such as 'worry', 'anxiety' or 'feeling empty'.
- **Mimicking the symptoms of dementia** Older people may show signs of withdrawal, memory loss and confusion that give rise to fears of dementia. Suspiciousness and paranoid thoughts are also more common in people who are severely depressed.
- **Types of depression** The bipolar form of the illness is unlikely to develop in older age for the first time. Manic episodes, found in the bipolar type, are often characterised by irritability and agitation. Minor depression is the most common form, probably triggered by external causes. Mood deterioration linked to other, physical illnesses and medication are also common.
- **Suicide** In older people the risk of suicide attempts decreases but the number of successful actions increases. Relevant figures are not easily available because research studies have not always looked at a representative number of older people. However, a report by Dr Cattell published in the journal *Advances in Psychiatric Treatment* in 2000 indicated that males over the age of 75 have the highest risk of suicide of any age group in nearly all industrialised countries.

Other contributing factors

The following list draws attention to a range of 'situations' that often play an underlying role. They are unlikely to cause depression by themselves, but they might influence the course of illness if they occur in combination with other elements. This list may help carers to gain a fuller picture if they discreetly observe their relative's behaviour and monitor moods and physical health.

- **Loneliness** Living alone in itself is unlikely to make a person depressed, especially if the person either likes, or has become accustomed to, their own company. Nevertheless, in this type of situation feelings of loneliness may develop as other depressive symptoms become worse. For example, someone who has never lived alone and has recently lost a partner may be affected more by their solitary circumstances.

- **Worry and anxiety** Some people are constant worriers and the pattern may have grown into a habit over the years because mulling over an issue is a great way to pass the time or trigger a conversation. Excessive worrying is not a problem unless the two conditions – worry and depression – are affecting each other. Depression has the potential to increase worry and anxiety to uncomfortable levels. Conversely, a marked growth in obvious 'worry-time' might be a signal that depression is developing. The co-existence between depression and anxiety is well recognised by health professionals who work with older people.
- **Confusion and memory loss** It has been pointed out elsewhere that depression is not *directly* linked to dementia, although there are no guarantees that some form of dementia will not develop in the future. Doctors specialising in the care of older people are quite firm in their belief that the symptoms of depression are not signs of impending insanity or dementia. The Royal College of Psychiatrists advises families and friends to 'reassure [their relative] that they are not "going senile" or demented'. This positive information has helped many relatives and older people to cope with a bout of depression.
- **Fear of dementia** While some of the symptoms of depression (for example, forgetfulness and feeling confused) might appear similar to the early stages of dementia, there are important differences. The type of memory loss found in dementia is permanent, whereas the memory loss associated with depression is short lived. Also, people with Alzheimer's disease are usually unaware that they have lost their memory powers, whereas depressed people are only too well aware that something is wrong. According to the Royal College of Psychiatrists, tests given to people with depression generally show that memory function remains very good and is certainly similar to that of their peers. Unfortunately, the phenomenon is liable to be self-generating, in that the short term effect of memory loss is to create worry. The problem is then made worse by agitation and anxiety which, in turn, make it harder for people to pay attention to what is happening around them and retain the information in their memory.

■ **Loss of appetite and poor sleep patterns** These are common examples of physical symptoms of depression which are also found in other disorders. Because of this, the doctor examining your relative is likely to ask questions and make checks in order to rule out, or reveal, other undiagnosed illnesses. Health professionals are aware that older people are more likely to focus on their physical symptoms, rather than emotional distress, as many people in this generation were brought up to believe that it is distasteful to mention mental health problems. An obsessive focus on physical problems could be a ploy to hide the fact that something else is bothering them.

Reluctance to seek help

It is possible if you are reading this book, that the person you are caring for has already been diagnosed as having depression. If this is not the case, however, it cannot be over-stated that depression is an illness that can be treated. Encourage your relative to visit their own doctor as soon as possible if you both feel their symptoms need professional attention. According to the mental health charities, many older people are reluctant to ask for help because there is a stigma attached to this type of illness and they mistakenly believe that it is a personal problem rather than an illness.

Rhoda

'My mother put forward a number of excuses before she agreed to go to the surgery. She said she was not entitled to support, that there are no cures and that she would be taking up the doctor's valuable time.'

Alex

'My father kept repeating that it was a cross he had to bear. His father had suffered from depression and I know that the family had not understood the illness well.'

If your relative is showing reluctance to seek professional help, listen to their arguments as it helps to assess their frame of mind. Discuss the options without dismissing their reasoning and treat their views sensitively as they will feel very real to them. The arguments may be a smokescreen that is hiding a great deal of fear. Be aware also that the depression itself will make them feel lethargic and reduce their ability to think logically. If possible, gradually work your way towards an agreement that the doctor is the best person to give an opinion. Bear in mind that most people faced with this situation would be very nervous. Reassure them that you will accompany them to the surgery and, if they wish, be in the consulting room to speak directly to the doctor (or ask a sympathetic friend to help). Be prepared to do lots of listening. Tell them that by admitting there might be a problem and seeking help they are being very brave; it is not a waste of the doctor's time. Statistics show that the average GP will see at least one person in every surgery session who complains of being depressed, so the vast majority of doctors will have had a great deal of practice at responding in a supportive way. Many doctors have received special training in dealing with depression, and are experienced in recognising the varied and sometimes disguised symptoms described by their older patients.

Specialist services

The GP is a gatekeeper for all sorts of other services that specialise in mental health problems, many of which are particularly well equipped for dealing with older people. For example:

- community psychiatric nurses, who visit people at home, are often based at GP surgeries;
- social workers, who make an assessment and arrange for practical support and personal care (it is possible that depression in some older people is made worse by their anxiety about taking care of themselves);
- day centres and lunch clubs, which are available in most areas of the country, offering a nutritious meal and social activities;

■ voluntary sector support covering a wide variety of services: information, advice, counselling, befriending, telephone helplines and day care. (However, the full range of services is unlikely to be offered in all parts of the country, particularly in rural areas.)

Information about the wide variety of services, how to gain access to the social care system and an explanation of the assessment procedures are described more fully in Chapter 6.

Treatments

The range of treatments has already been covered fully in Chapter 2. To recap, the main treatments for depression found in people at any age are:

■ medication using antidepressant tablets;
■ talking therapies which include counselling and psychological therapies;
■ electro-convulsive therapy (ECT) which, according to the Depression Alliance, is well tolerated by older people and may work better for them than for younger people;
■ light therapy;
■ self-help methods;
■ complementary therapies (covered in more detail in Chapter 8).

The methods chosen for treating older people will be no different to those already described in the list above. It is likely that a combination of methods will be used to enable your relative to remain as independent as possible, either at home or within safe, care-home surroundings, whichever is most appropriate. The GP will discuss the choices available and together you and your relative can decide which treatments are most appropriate.

It is worth noting that antidepressant tablets work as efficiently when taken by older people as with younger age groups. It is likely, however, that they will take longer to become effective – perhaps as long as six or eight weeks. Encourage your relative to continue taking the tablets for long enough to feel the benefits.

Safety with medicines

James, general practitioner

'Taking responsibility for their relative's drug regime is a job that many carers have to undertake. If you don't understand about any treatment, you can ask whoever is around, the doctor, the community psychiatric nurse or the pharmacist at your local chemist.'

It is just as important that care is taken in the administration of anti-depressants as it would be for any other drugs. Professional people will give you considerable support but it is probable that you will also have to take responsibility for certain aspects of your relative's care. If there is any chance that they might be confused about which drugs to take, or how much, or that they might not take their drugs at all, do not leave any form of medication out for them to take later. The correct dosage must be supervised. If your relative is able to take their drugs safely but has difficulty opening containers, ask a pharmacist for details of specially designed tablet boxes with separate compartments into which you can load a day's supply. If you are concerned about getting the timing and doses right (perhaps because your relative is taking several drugs) it might help to write out a chart as a memory aid for yourself and them.

The following basic rules apply to any medication:

■ Check the label to ensure you have been given the correct drug – mistakes do occasionally occur;

■ follow the instructions given on the label;

■ never stop using a prescribed drug without taking medical advice;

■ take the dose regularly, at the stated times, to achieve the intended result;

■ always tell the GP (or pharmacist for over-the-counter medicines) about all other medication being taken;

■ never take more than the prescribed dose – if the symptoms persist or become worse, or side effects are a problem, seek advice;

■ store all medicines in a secure, locked place away from children and any person who may not handle the drugs safely.

Note **In the case of antidepressants if a dose is delayed for a few hours take it as soon as it is remembered. If the timing is close to when the next dose is due, take that alone without trying to catch up. Never double up on doses.**

Suicide threats

A belief that life is no longer worth living is often felt by many older people with depression so do not be surprised if your relative expresses views like this. Common reasons include deep misery at being alone (even if this is untrue); feeling futile and full of suffering; despair because they have an incurable disorder (mental and/or physical) and, for some people with a psychiatric illness, imaginary voices suggesting suicide. Articulating the depth of their emotions is likely to be very difficult for your relative as their innermost thoughts might be in quite a turmoil: severe distress and fear; shame and humility; a struggle to be brave and perhaps a longing to join a loved one who is already dead. It is better for you to be forewarned and ready to deal with this situation and it might help if you think through your own feelings in advance.

A leading mental health charity has said that people rarely commit suicide in the peak of a depression, but the risk increases when they start to recover as this is when they rediscover the energy and direction to form a brooding suicide plan. The recovery may be brought about through treatment, or may be spontaneous, but the cause makes little difference to the thought processes that accompany it. In some cases, people were even found to have deliberately misled their friends and family about their progress in order to carry out a suicide plan without raising suspicion.

Jen, whose father took an overdose

'I thought things were improving ever so slightly, as my father began to be less withdrawn. We were deeply shocked when he took an overdose using pills he had been storing up. We did not realise that people with depression are more likely to resort to suicide in this very early recovery stage than they were before.'

Respond to your relative's negative statements with firm and positive replies. Use the arguments already covered earlier in the book; for example, that depression is common, treatable in all age groups and not shameful. Enlist the support of family and friends if possible. There are two good reasons for this. Firstly, your relative may benefit from additional attention and, secondly, you should not try to bear this burden alone. You can only do your best to offer help and support and cannot take complete responsibility for another person's actions. Above all, be clear that the doctor is the appropriate person to advise your relative.

Julia

'Without my carer I don't know how I would have coped. I probably wouldn't be here now.'

The following list offers ways to help you combat their despair.

- Listen sympathetically and never dismiss their feelings as nonsense.
- Ask why they are feeling so low at that particular time.
- Encourage them to continue with any treatment methods.
- Tell them clearly that the depression will improve and that they are not 'going mad'.
- Avoid being too jolly.
- Always take threats of suicide seriously.
- If you suspect that suicide is being considered, probe gently into how deep their intention might be, whether they have

already tried any form of self-harm and whether they are secretly planning the means to such an end; for example, have they hidden a store of tablets.

Agnes

'After my mother took an overdose I understood that she was more depressed than I had realised. I had been busy with my own life and thought that she was getting over the death of my father. I now make myself more readily available to listen to her feelings and we have all told her that people care deeply about her well-being. It isn't easy because she seems to demand lots of reassurance.'

June

'As a carer I often found it hard to know how much advice to give and how much action I should take on my partner's behalf. I eventually found that the best kind of help enabled my partner to make the decisions for himself but when he got really bad and started talking about suicide, I sought professional help.'

Depression Alliance

'Relatives should be aware of the financial implications of suicide. To our knowledge, no insurance policy will cover suicide. We have heard of many cases where dependents of people who have committed suicide are left penniless as well as grief-stricken.'

Emergency action

In the event that you find your relative in a semi-conscious or unconscious state – for whatever reason – telephone for an emergency ambulance immediately by dialling 999 and then follow the guidelines for giving first aid (see page 85). Deal with any obvious dangers such as turning off a gas supply, and take a note of the situation as you will be questioned about the incident. Keep any evidence that might be to hand; for example, there may be tablets close by or some form of poisonous substance. If the person you are caring for is no longer alive, telephone their surgery for help and you will be advised about how to proceed. If the surgery is shut it is likely that you will be redirected to an 'emergency call service' where a trained operator will take the details.

For more *i*nformation

i The Samaritans offer emotional support to people who feel isolated, in despair and suicidal. The telephone lines are open and staffed by trained counsellors 24 hours daily.

i For carers who have access to the Internet, a huge range of websites are available dealing with depression. There are far too many to illustrate here and not all offer a permanent service. However, one example of a site worth investigating is STAND, at www.depression.org, which offers users a range of information and facilities about anxiety and depression, covering editorial comment, chat rooms, book reviews and self-help advice.

Social support

This type of support is not classed as a treatment, although taking a look at the practical and social aspects of your relative's lifestyle is a useful exercise to undertake. People at any age can become more depressed if they are not able to deal confidently with daily living. For an older person, the ability to take corrective measures to improve their circumstances may feel like a huge step. Examples that exacerbate depression might include:

- living in difficult conditions in a home that is no longer suitable, eg too many stairs;
- feeling unsafe because they live in a dangerous neighbourhood;
- feeling isolated and lonely;
- no longer being able to take care of personal hygiene and cook nourishing meals;

■ losing the ability to keep their home or their garden clean and tidy.

Advice and practical help can be obtained from the appropriate agency, depending on the nature of the problem. You could try:

■ a social worker who will offer guidance about most social situations (see page 56);
■ the housing department at the local council offices (see telephone directory);
■ the Citizens Advice Bureau (see telephone directory);
■ a depression-related charity such as Depression Alliance (see page 207).

A word of caution: it would be unwise to instigate any significant changes such as moving neighbourhoods or into a care home (which might later be regretted) while your relative is still in the throes of depression. Major decisions should be made only when the depression has lifted or it is clear that they will be unable to remain independent.

Dealing with the effects of a bereavement

This section is aimed at those carers who believe that their relative's depression is especially aggravated by a recent bereavement. It offers brief background advice only and is not intended to be a comprehensive guide on dealing with a bereaved person. For more information, the national charity CRUSE – Bereavement Care (see page 207) offers information, support and encouragement to bereaved people and their families.

For any person, the term 'bereavement' means more than the loss of a loved one. It encompasses a wide range of life-type experiences involving the loss of something they hold dear such as their independence, a useful or satisfying role, financial security, a well-loved family home, etc. Older people are thought to be more at risk of suffering the effects of bereavement because they are likely to be exposed to many such life-events, often in quick succession.

Professional people describe this phenomenon as 'bereavement overload'.

How people mourn

Bereaved people describe similar feelings and often experience phases of grief that have been identified as common to most people. The way people show their grief is a personal matter, so it is inaccurate to lump everyone into a category whereby all bereaved people follow a stereotypical set of stages. However, it does appear that most people go through the same broad process so at some point your relative's emotions and behaviour are likely to be similar to those listed below:

- feelings of shock, numbness, pain, disbelief;
- feelings of fear, guilt, anger, resentment;
- signs of withdrawal, apathy, quietness, lack of interest;
- expressions of bargaining, searching, questioning, yearning, wanting to 'put the clock back';
- signs and symptoms of depression, emptiness, deep anxiety, overwhelming sense of loss, over-dependence;
- expressions and signs of acceptance, recognition, relief, moving forward, recovery.

While your relative is going through the early stages of bereavement, do not expect them to move forward very quickly. Anticipate, accept and even encourage outward signs of emotion. Take each day at a time: it is not uncommon to move forwards and backwards along a continuum of grief. Gently introduce the view that meaningful life did not necessarily finish on a certain day in the past when their loved one died. Pose the question 'what would … have wanted you to do'? Suggest that that their loved one might want to give them permission to get better, and help them to find reasons to let go of the past. Be clear that moving forward is not about forgetting their past life together, or about being disloyal to a memory. Rather, it is about cherishing old times in a realistic way.

There are a small number of people who become fixed in their sorrow to such an extent that their grief cannot be resolved. There is a distinct difference between the observance of mourning rituals that take place after the death and the onset of a prolonged period of mourning that shows no signs of abating. If you believe that this might be a significant factor affecting your relative's state of mind, it is important that you do not struggle on alone. Seek advice about how to deal with the situation from a specialist counsellor (see CRUSE – Bereavement Care above).

Conclusion

There is still a significant number of older people from the 'polite generation', individuals who grew up during a period when it was not fashionable to discuss their emotions and when people who valued 'society's' opinion would not feel able to acknowledge that they or anyone connected with them might have a mental health problem. If your relative is mature in years, it is very possible they will have views like these, and this might prevent them from acknowledging their own problems. Harbouring such notions or acting in this manner is not wrong, it's simply different to the way many younger people behave. As a carer you can help your relative to adjust to their illness, support them through their treatment, listen repeatedly to their woes, be patient if they refuse to be helped and rejoice with them when they feel better.

It is often a relative or friend who first notices depression in an older person and is their main source of support. This role can be exhausting for relatives and often frustrating. Try to share the load if possible amongst family members and friends and don't be embarrassed or stubborn about seeking support and respite time for yourself. Chapter 4 concentrates on the carer's role and Chapter 8 offers a range of ways to relieve stress.

4 The caring role

The term 'carer' is used to mean anyone who spends time and energy looking after someone in need of extra attention because of their age or physical or other disability. This could be a friend or neighbour, but is most likely to be a close relative. The word 'carer' in this context is intended to denote an 'informal' or 'non-professional' person, rather than a trained worker. This chapter offers support and guidance to help you in your role of carer.

Becoming a carer may lay you open to some strong, and perhaps confusing, feelings and it may take a while for you to adjust. Taking on a caring role, particularly where this involves caring for someone you love dearly, is not something you set out to do, like a professional job with ample training. Families enter into a caring relationship in one of a number of ways: perhaps very swiftly, following the dramatic diagnosis of an acute illness or a stroke; more gradually, as the health of a relative with an existing illness deteriorates; or simply because their relative can no longer manage alone. Whatever the underlying reason for your taking on this role, you may also find that, simultaneously, your relative develops a depressive illness.

What does it mean to be a carer?

In general terms, caring varies from a full-time activity if someone is seriously ill to as little as keeping a regular eye on a relative's daily affairs. The aim of most carers is to help the less able person to remain in their own home, leading as stress free and independent a life as possible for as long as they can. Wherever your position on the spectrum of care, it is likely that you are undertaking many of the following:

Fact Box

- Over six million people in the UK look after a relative or friend who cannot manage without help because of illness, frailty or disability.
- More women – 3.9 million (18 per cent) – than men – 2.9 million (14 per cent) are carers.
- The peak age for becoming a carer is between 45 to 64 years (25 per cent of adults in this age group).
- Estimates suggest there may be 51,000 carers aged 16 years or under – most of them care for a parent.
- The financial costs of caring are significant and the support is paltry. *Carers' Allowance* (available to certain carers) is one of the lowest welfare benefits of its kind; 77 per cent of carers who responded to a survey by Carers UK claimed to be financially 'worse off'.
- Six out of ten carers in one study felt that caring was affecting their own health. A further study found that over 20 per cent of carers, providing over 20 hours of care a week, had a mental health problem themselves.
- CarersLine (see page 205) receives approximately 20,000 enquiries per year.

Source: Facts about Carers, published by Carers UK, May 2003

- providing a safe and comfortable home;
- doing practical jobs such as shopping, cooking, cleaning, laundry and gardening;
- giving personal care and carrying out basic nursing procedures;
- offering love, emotional support and company;
- providing help and advice on running personal affairs;
- reducing isolation and bringing a bit of the 'outside world' into the daily life of someone who may be mentally ill.

Recognising yourself as a carer

Jeanne

'When Sam was diagnosed with depression I felt so numb and was shocked that the doctor called it a mental health illness – I couldn't think about what to do next. When he was first unwell I never called myself a carer.'

You may not think of yourself as a carer because you undertake your tasks out of love and friendship, and you may have fallen into the caring role because no-one else is available. Many carers do not recognise themselves as such and therefore do not seek information or know where to look for further help. Now that your relative has depression it is vital that you are aware of the support and help that is available and that, as a carer, you also have rights that go alongside the responsibilities. This chapter offers information, advice and support to anyone who cares in some way for a spouse, relative or friend. It cannot give you all of the answers or solve all of your problems but it may help you to understand better some of the issues faced by non-professional carers.

Stuart, a sufferer

'Loving care is a vital element in helping someone who is depressed. My carer supported me throughout by providing information, listening to me and sometimes just sitting quietly with me. There were times when I just wanted to be left alone and my carer respected that as well.'

There are an estimated 5.7 million carers in the UK (one in eight people), nearly two million of whom provide substantial amounts of care. At times, being a carer creates tremendous anxiety and distress; you may be undertaking tasks that feel difficult and unfamiliar, you are largely unpaid and untrained, and are often on duty for 24 hours each day seven days a week. You will need to:

- pace yourself;
- use a range of skills and experience;
- take on an enduring commitment;
- build up strong physical and mental systems;
- control your emotions;
- maintain a good sense of humour;
- wherever possible, find a means of receiving personal support.

All of this is rather a lot to expect from one untrained person! The responsibility will tax your patience and you won't always get it right. Life is never completely straightforward and you may feel that it has already dealt you a nasty blow. But there are many sources of advice and support you can draw upon to help you cope with very difficult situations and find ways of managing the stress.

Your perceptions and feelings as a carer

Tanya works as a carers' support worker

'Carers often feel tired and upset – these are normal reactions to your the situation. But if you begin to feel over-stressed, angry and weepy these powerful emotions may be a signal that that you need a short break. I realise it's easy to say "be calm", but lots of emotional energy can be spent worrying when it won't actually help.'

You will have your ups and downs and there will be days when you feel you cannot cope. Even if you chose your caring situation without hesitation this will not stop you from having negative feelings, and while many people decide to care willingly this will not be true of every carer. Professional people who work with carers understand that carers feel a range of very conflicting emotions, and that sometimes these will spill over and be directed both towards their relative and towards the people who offer them support. Anger, frustration, fear, resentment and guilt will often exist alongside other emotions such as sadness, love, anxiety and concern. Powerful emotions can drain and exhaust you so try not to add 'worry' to the list. Worry and guilt are two emotions that cause much wasted energy. Look instead at problems from a different angle: if you feel in control, you will cope well; if the problem is not within your control, spending time being worried or guilty won't improve the situation and may even prevent you from finding a solution. Carers frequently bottle up strong emotions to protect others, but everyone needs an outlet for themselves. Letting go of unhappy feelings is better than storing them up.

Tom, a carer

'I sometimes felt angry with her, wondering why she couldn't pull herself together. I blamed her for her illness when really I was angry with myself for not being able to help.'

'Carers should remember they too are human, and they have the right both to feel vulnerable and to express their emotions.'

Sizing up the problem

It is still assumed in society today that a blood-tie or marriage relationship automatically makes a person (usually the woman in the partnership) the main carer and that, in this role, she or he must undertake a number of onerous, unpaid tasks. You may believe this yourself. It may be assumed by others that you have the ability to cope and that your capacity to care can stretch to meet all the demands that are placed upon you. You may feel that other people expect so much from you – family members, doctors, social workers and nurses – and that you cannot let them down.

To help you come to terms with your role of as a carer, it is important that you think about all of these expectations, including what you expect of yourself. If you feel confused or overwhelmed by the enormity of the task, talking to someone – perhaps another carer or a counsellor from a mental health centre – might help. Look at the list below and tick off those feelings that have crossed your mind in recent weeks:

- I lack confidence and feel inadequate;
- I have no qualifications to do the job;
- I am worried about shortage of money;
- I lack recognition/status;
- I am not sure where to turn for allies or support;
- I am bewildered by the maze of services;
- I am unclear about what I can ask for;
- I feel my needs are always disregarded in favour of the 'patient';
- I have no time or space to be myself;
- Who cares for me?

These thoughts are very common, even if they have been only fleeting. Don't block them out. Accept that occasionally carers do feel unable to carry on; that carers themselves may become depressed if they over do it and sometimes they feel forced to take dramatic steps to make their voices heard. Support workers should do everything in their power to ease your position and avert a crisis. However, although risks can be minimised, a crisis can never be completely ruled out. Unfortunately, not all carers have access to an adequate, informal support system. If this applies to you, do speak to your GP or the duty social worker at your closest social services office and ask about additional help before crisis point is reached.

Setting boundaries

Sara, who works as a carers' support worker

'Many people become carers without being aware that carers have rights to services and that they do have choices about their situation.'

How did you become a carer? Did it creep up on you slowly as your relative's mental health got worse, or were you thrust into the role suddenly because of a crisis? Whatever the original reason, at some point it is vital that you sit back and take stock of the current situation. Ask yourself a few searching questions and think logically and seriously about the answers. Perhaps an unbiased listener will help you sort out your feelings? If so, phone a helpline and talk to a counsellor. You can use CarersLine on 0808 808 7777 or a mental health charity (see page 212).

Ask yourself the following questions:

- Why am I doing this job?
- Will I feel that I have rejected someone I love if I stop?
- Is the caring situation going to be long term or short term?
- Am I being pressured by other people?
- Do I want to continue or pass the responsibility over to others?
- What are my options for change?

As a carer you must make a conscious decision about whether to continue with caring or not, because making a definite choice will increase your mental strength help you to cope with the task – however difficult it might be. There may be times when carers feel in despair, but when they perceive that they have no choice, that they were pressured into the situation by others or that they did not fully consider the seriousness of the situation before it over-took them, they are more likely to become angry, resentful and suffer ill health. There is nothing wrong with saying 'no' if you already feel over burdened. If you cannot continue to care for your relative at home, you can still continue to be involved with their day to day care.

How 'good' is your caring situation?

> **Rhoda**
>
> 'As my mother's health got worse and I took over more of the responsi-bility for her day to day care. I lived around the corner so it was easy to stop by to and from work. We took each stage at a time and my mother and I talked honestly about how things were going.'

Researchers studying informal caring, given by close relatives, have identified a model of a *good* caring situation that is recog-nised by professional people as an important factor in maintaining a positive experience for the key people involved. While acknowl-edging that no caring situation can hope to fulfil the ideal all of the time, it is important that everyone accepts the value of such a model and works towards achieving *some* of the suggestions.

The list below can be seen as a 'model list' for a caring situation:

- The carer makes a conscious choice whether or not to care.
- The carer is able to recognise their own limits and needs.
- The carer lives close by, but not necessarily in the same house.
- A network of care is set up, so that responsibility is shared.
- Carers have time to themselves and don't have to give up most of their own life.

- Carers have access to information and help to learn skills.
- A good past relationship existed between the carer and the person being cared for.
- The dependent person wishes to stay as independent as possible.
- The dependent person retains their own friends.
- The carer fosters independence in the dependent person.
- Everybody keeps a sense of humour.
- Professional help is there when it is needed.
- The carer feels supported and valued.

Caring specifically for someone with depression

Living with (or supporting) someone who is depressed can be more taxing that helping someone over a physical illness. People who are depressed tend to believe that no one else can help – they may be cold, aloof and refuse all offers of comfort. However much you all love each other, a person who is ill with depression can cause deep feelings of frustration and anger within the family, especially when practical efforts and physical love are rejected. And you, the main carer, may be at the centre of this turmoil. Don't be upset if this frustration then turns to guilt at the thought of being angry with someone who is clearly unwell. Families often express powerlessness at their inability to help lift the black clouds and are fearful of what the outcome might be. Some relatives are also concerned for their own mental health state, living in close proximity to so much negativity. They may even begin to wonder whether depression might be catching.

The simple answer to this question is 'No'. Depression is not actually passed on from one person to another in the same way that an infectious disease can be 'caught', although a gloomy atmosphere may influence the mood of others. If there is a history of depressive illness running through a family, however, then relatives should be aware of their own vulnerability and take some self-help measures.

Many people who are prone to depression can easily recognise their own warning symptoms. If you are affected by dealing with a depressed relative you should take medical advice.

Despite worries about how useful they can be, the family and friends of a depressed person can play a significant role in helping them recover. Here are a few tips to help you gauge your level of response.

- Be a good listener. Never under estimate the value of being around to listen (positively). You can do this by acknowledging your relative's pain, encouraging hope, agreeing that you may not understand how they feel and firmly repeating that their depression will eventually lift.
- Give them a sense that you are sharing their worries without sharing their bleak view of their health and the future. It is also important that you protect yourself, so in your mind set a time limit for discussing their feelings and then quietly edge the conversation round towards more general matters.
- Spend some extra time with your relative, boost their confidence and make them feel special. Try to set some goals that are specific and realistic. You could write these down and go back to them after a week or so and review how well they have moved forward.
- Encourage them to be active and stimulated by what is going on around them, perhaps by joining them for a walk or listening to music.
- Don't use bullying tactics even though you may feel frustrated by their lack of effort. A calm, firm manner is better, both for you and for them, otherwise you may both end up feeling upset.
- Do be open and honest as depressed people appreciate directness and frankness. They certainly don't wish to feel that everyone is treating them with suspicion or keeping secrets.
- Reassure them that their depression will end and that it is treatable. In some way, try to put their feelings into perspective and reduce their sense of isolation.

- Be prepared to repeat your tactics over and over again as depressed people are easily swayed by internal worry and doubt. Maybe you can identify any factors that are hindering progression?
- In practical terms, make sure your relative is eating sufficient food, taking care of personal hygiene and not resorting to excessive alcohol.
- Don't be over protective because dissuading someone from taking risks can dampen their self-confidence.
- Be wary of overdoing the advice and mentioning the depression unnecessarily, especially when recovery is clearly under way.

What formal support is available for carers?

Increasingly, the rights and needs of carers are being taken into account, although it has taken many years of lobbying by pressure groups and individuals to introduce the changes in legislation we have now arrived at. A number of Acts of Parliament have been passed, and local charters produced, to secure and highlight the rights of carers and disabled people. The most relevant pieces of legislation are summarised here. If you need a more detailed explanation of the rights and services to which you are entitled, you should contact your local social services department (social work department in Scotland) which will be listed in the telephone directory.

State provision

NHS and Community Care Act 1990

The NHS and Community Care Act is designed to help meet the care needs of older people, those with learning and physical disabilities and mental health problems, preferably in their own home or the area where they live. Social services take the lead role and work together with the NHS and voluntary organisations to offer a broad range of services for people in need and their carers. The services cannot promise to meet all needs, because community care is subject to certain eligibility criteria (see pages125–129) but a trained person, called a care manager, will assess the needs of the person you care for and then, if that person is eligible, arrange appropriate services in what is known as a 'care package'. The services (care package) arranged through social services are means tested.

Carers' (Recognition and Services) Act 1995

This Act came into force on 1 April 1996. It defines a carer as 'someone who provides (or intends to provide) a substantial amount of care on a regular basis', including children and young people under the age of 18 years. It contains two main elements that deal with the rights of carers: to ask for a separate assessment of their care needs when the person they care for is being assessed or reassessed; and the duty of local authorities to take into consideration the findings of this assessment when deciding which services to offer the person being cared for (see Chapter 6).

The Act requires social services departments, if requested to do so by a carer, to assess the ability of a carer to provide and/or to continue to provide care, and take this care into account when deciding what services to provide to the person being cared for. To qualify for an assessment, a carer must be providing (or intending to provide) regular and substantial care, and the person they care for must be assessed by social services at the same time. Because there is no official definition of 'regular' and 'substantial', each caring situation will be assessed individually. The assessment should recognise the carer's knowledge of the person, and the responsibility for the caring situation should be agreed as a shared undertaking between the carer and the social services department.

Carers National Association

'The Carers' (Recognition and Services) Act 1995 has been one of the most significant developments in the history of the carers' movement. Not only did it recognise the rights of carers for the first time, but the campaign which led to the Carers' Act showed the level of agreement there was about the rights and needs of carers.'

Charters

Most social services departments have published charters in recent years, which aim to tell people what they can expect from the agencies that provide 'community care' services for adults. These charters, across the country, have been given the collective title 'Better Care – Higher Standards'. The various charters have been drawn up to reflect the standards and targets that have been set by health care trusts, social services and housing departments in order to fulfil local need, so the content will differ slightly from area to area. Basically, however, the charters fall into two types, which are summarised below. Contact your social services office to enquire about local versions.

Charters for Carers

These charters usually acknowledge the valuable role carers perform in caring for someone at home. They state that practical help is a key priority for social services departments and set out how the department aims to respond to typical requests expressed by carers. The charters offer:

- opportunities for sharing experiences;
- recognition for carers;
- practical help;
- information and advice;
- advice about welfare benefits;
- a short break from caring.

Community Care Charters

These charters complement the Community Care Plan and are concerned with the services that help people to remain in their own homes. They cover:

- being able to get in touch;
- understanding people's needs;
- planning care;
- unmet needs;

■ the services people can expect to receive;
■ how to access information;
■ what to do if things go wrong;
■ relationships with people receiving services.

Both types of charter will be concerned with telling people about the services they can expect to receive for home care, personal help and care in care homes, and how they can gain access to services more easily. Older people will also be represented on the independent, statutory patients' forum, set up from 2002 in every health trust area, so patients can have their say about how local NHS services are run.

Carers' support centres and workers

Tanya (a carers' support worker)

'Before you meet a professional person jot down a few notes as it's important to ask the questions that are right for you. Try not to make assumptions about what you think may be available – people are often surprised at the amount of services that exist.'

There are many schemes set up around the country specifically to provide help and support for carers. They are run mainly by health and social services teams and voluntary organisations. The workers understand the problems and feelings of isolation experienced by carers and are specially trained to help carers receive relevant and up to date information, gain access to services and welfare benefits and guide them in their caring role. Support workers welcome contact with you as a carer and will listen to your hopes, concerns and fears. Many produce newsletters, run local support groups for carers and have drop-in and respite care facilities.

Sara (a carers' support worker)

'We understand that carers get to the end of their tether and may be quite close to physical and mental collapse at times; occasionally it is their relative who takes the brunt of their anxieties and anger. Tension is usually relieved through shouting but carers can lose their temper more violently. If you feel it's time to look at ways of relieving the strain then do seek help before you reach crisis point. If you feel really desperate then give the Samaritans a call.'

Your own needs as a carer

Jeanne

'Although my husband's needs come first I do think about myself as well. If I couldn't function he would suffer so I try to rest when he is asleep, and I sit with him and we eat together.'

Don't ignore your own health and well-being. This may sound like a tall order but you do need to maintain your own strength.

- Eat regularly and properly – if you are preparing meals for someone else try not to skimp on your own food.
- Take regular breaks from caring, even if you only find time to walk in the garden or read a book. Plan longer breaks at regular intervals.
- Arrange time away from the house to meet other people because isolation can be a major problem for many carers. There are sitting services available that will send a volunteer to stay with your relative – try your local Age Concern group or your local branch of the charity Crossroads (see page 206).
- Learn to move your relative safely, because strained and injured backs are a great problem for people who are suddenly thrust into a caring role. Ask your community nurse or social worker about how to do this.

■ Take cat naps during the day if your night time sleep is disturbed. And don't feel guilty!

■ Ask about help with housework or gardening if you are overtired. Some local councils and voluntary organisations run volunteer gardening schemes.

Talking about feelings

One of the difficulties faced by carers is how to talk to a relative about their having a mental illness. Likewise, the problem of how to communicate with their family may also be bothering the person who is suffering from depression. In truth, depression remains a topic that many people find awkward to broach and have difficulty discussing. There seems to be a 'code' that governs where and when sensitive subjects are introduced – for example, not in front of the person with the illness, nor within earshot of younger children. Carers and patients often find it easier to talk about their depression with professional people than with members of their own family; however, even doctors and nurses are not always comfortable answering questions and giving information.

Many carers express a desire to simply 'talk to someone' but often they don't know where to start or even whether they ought to be discussing their relative's illness. But talking about difficult subjects can be very beneficial, so despite your possible dread of talking about depression try to overcome your reluctance by helping each other describe how you individually feel.

What can be gained by talking? Probably, at least some of the following:

■ support for each other;
■ comfort and a sense of togetherness;
■ reduction of fear and isolation;
■ openness and agreement about ground rules for behaviour;
■ a sense of perspective;
■ clarity and answers to questions;
■ regaining and/or retaining a sense of control;

- the sharing of information;
- correction of myths;
- a better chance to find solutions to problems.

The list could be longer – perhaps you and your relative can add some benefits that you have gained by talking about their depression. If you need a listening ear from outside your immediate circle, there are many other people and organisations to whom you can turn for support (see page 202–218).

How to share feelings

Emily

'My husband and I are very close and we have never found it difficult to talk about issues – until he had depression. Once we got over our reticence we both agreed that it was fear of the unknown that held us back.'

There are no rules or special phrases which deal with the topic and make everyone feel less inhibited. But the following guidelines may be useful:

- Behave in a sensitive and responsible manner, agreeing that matters spoken about privately remain confidential and details will only be passed on with express permission. For example, you could say 'May I share this information with ...?'
- Let your relative set the pace if this feels easier.
- Acknowledge the open expression of feelings, such as tears or anger, and be supportive, but don't attempt to stop the flow of emotion prematurely as most outbursts of this nature tend to subside naturally after the emotion has been vented.
- If you are having a bad day try to explain what you are feeling and why. For example, 'I feel low today because ...' is much easier to understand than a withdrawn manner.
- Expression of strong emotions is neither right nor wrong. But being offered the opportunity to express emotions is important.

- Give each other a chance to respond, whether with words or without. A good hug or sitting in shared silence may be sufficient.
- Don't be frightened of speaking about the past or the future.

Talking to children

Talking to children about the illness of a close relative will be a painful task that one family member must be prepared to take on. Children are often very perceptive and quick to pick up on family problems. However distressing it may be, it is better for the children to be told at an early stage and then kept informed. Ask a health professional for help if this would make the job easier as they can advise you about how best to introduce the subject in an appropriate way. Talk to each child at a level that is right for their own emotional development, which may differ from that of other children in a peer or family group. Anyone given the responsibility of speaking to children should know them well because it is important to be aware of their reaction. It is also important to answer children's questions truthfully and simply, avoiding euphemisms which may be misunderstood. Even very young children will be aware if a parent or close family member has a serious illness, and will worry if no explanation is given. Children need to know how the person's illness will affect their own life and routine, and their routine should be disrupted as little as possible. It may be necessary to repeat the information several times and be prepared to return to the subject as often as the child wishes, however upsetting this may feel for the adult.

Children have the right to be treated with respect and to be covered by the same code of confidentiality afforded to adults. Members of the wider family should be aware of what each child knows as the children may approach others for confirmation. It is not fair to give a child false hope or inaccurate information to save an adult distress, so the information that is given should be honest and consistent. Take great care to assure any children involved that they are not in any way to blame for the illness, as depression is a disease that affects many people without anyone being at fault.

Children may also need particular support and understanding following a bereavement. Often this is difficult for those left behind, as they can be so wrapped up in their own grief. Special counselling is available for bereaved children. Your community psychiatric nurse, GP or health visitor should be able to tell you what is available in your area.

For more *i*nformation

i CRUSE – Bereavement Care (see page 207 for address) offers bereavement counselling for children and adults.

Respite care and practical support

Help is provided to carers by the care services (see Chapter 6). Most care homes offer respite to carers, either through admission or a day care service. They are able to offer psychosocial support to carers, and help through the apparent maze of the statutory social services. There are many other self-help groups and voluntary organisations offering support to carers in the form of sitting services and specialist support groups.

Practical support is also important. Advice about where to get pieces of equipment sometimes gets overlooked because the professional person is focusing on the patient and maybe assumes that the carer knows. Information and practical guidance about such procedures as moving your relative safely are best covered by the appropriate professional person at the time of need. Examples of useful caring aids are included in Chapter 6. If you are unsure about where to go for equipment, or feel you do not have the skills to undertake a nursing procedure, do ask for help rather than continue to struggle.

Emergency help and first aid

Carers often express fears about what to do if there is an accident and their relative falls. The advice from the Ambulance Service is to dial 999 for help. Do not attempt to move the person more than necessary as they will need to be assessed for injury.

If a situation occurs that needs prompt first aid, try to think and act calmly. You will be more effective and better able to reassure your relative. If your relative falls, collapses or becomes seriously ill, either call an ambulance yourself or ask someone to do this for you. Then treat your relative according to their state of consciousness, until help arrives.

If the person is conscious:

- reassure them that help is on the way;
- if they have difficulty breathing or complain of chest pains, gently raise them to a half sitting position, with the head and shoulders supported;
- if they feel faint, make sure that they are lying down and encourage them to take a few deep breaths (but not to over-breathe because this can quickly cause dizziness for other reasons);
- do not move a person who has fallen unless you absolutely have to, as this may cause further injury;
- if your relative has diabetes (as well as depression) give them a sugary drink or a sugar lump or other sweet food;
- do *not* give anything to eat or drink if your relative does not have diabetes.

If the person is unconscious:

- if possible, lie them on the floor on their side; otherwise try to position the head with the jaw forwards in order to maintain a clear airway and to prevent saliva and the tongue from falling backwards;
- loosen tight clothing;

- cover the person with a blanket to keep them warm;
- do _not_ try to remove dentures as doing so may cause more harm;
- do _not_ give any food or fluids of any kind.

If you become ill or need extra help

If you are ill yourself and need additional help at home during the day, you can contact the duty social services officer or your GP. For assistance outside office hours, contact the social services emergency duty team or a medical answering service. (Look up the numbers in the telephone directory and put them by the telephone now.)

Carer's emergency card

You might be concerned that you could have an accident or be taken ill while you are away from home, leaving the person you care for alone. You can obtain an emergency identity card that gives information about you as a carer so that your relative will not be left unattended. Cards are available from Carers UK (address on page 205).

Carers' advice line

A telephone helpline offering a wide range of information to carers operates nationally for the cost of a local call. Run by Carers UK, lines are open Monday to Friday from 10.00am – 12.00 noon, and 2.00 – 4.00pm. Contact CarersLine on 0808 808 7777.

Emergency help systems

Many local authorities and some charities operate an emergency call system that is linked via the telephone service to specially trained operators (it may not be available to everyone). A charge is usually made to help fund the system, which will vary from area to area. Ask for information at your relative's health centre or GP surgery.

For more *i*nformation

i Age Concern Factsheet 28 *Help with telephones.*

i Age Concern Factsheet 6 *Finding help at home.*

i Carers UK acts as the national voice of carers raising awareness and providing support, advice and a range of information booklets (see page 205 for address).

i Counsel and Care: offers free counselling, information and advice for older people and carers, including specialist advice about using independent agencies and the administration of trust funds for single payments such as respite care (see page 206 for address).

i Crossroads Care – the local schemes are part of a national network set up to provide practical help and support to older people, disabled people and their carers (see page 206 for address).

i Depression Alliance leaflets *'Friends and Family'* and *'Caring for Carers'*.

i The main charities dealing with depression (see list on page 207) offer a range of services to families of people with mental health problems.

i Books are regularly published offering information and support for carers. Check with support organisations for an up-to-date booklist or ask at your local bookshop.

Fact Box

- 1.7 million carers provide care for 20 hours or more every week. 27 per cent of these are aged 65 years or over.
- 70 per cent of those cared for are aged 65 years or over.
- 6 per cent of people cared for have a mental disability.
- 14 per cent of carers claim to have 'given up work to care'.
- 51 per cent of carers provide personal care to someone within their own home; 22 per cent administer medicines; 71 per cent give other practical help.

Source: Facts About Carers, published by Carers UK, May 2003

Conclusion

This chapter has offered information and advice to help you focus on your role as a carer and given you an insight into the nature of caring. It has focused on 'talking-style' support, whereas later chapters deal with everyday affairs and practical issues.

Reading some of this information may have been painful for you, especially if it raised uncomfortable questions that you found it difficult to answer. If you are one of the many carers who are unfamiliar with the official system, this chapter aims to encourage you to seek support and ask for an assessment of your caring situation. The statistics in the Fact Boxes give you a clear indication that you are not alone in the caring business. Take heart in the fact that the predicament of carers is now under open discussion and their efforts are being increasingly recognised and supported.

5 Maximising 'good' health

The chances are that as you read this chapter your relative is already past the stages outlined in the previous chapters, has completed the necessary tests and is receiving treatment. Or, better still, they are feeling brighter and picking up the threads of life again. This chapter offers information and advice to help you both move forward.

The main effects of depression were outlined in Chapters 1 and 2. Although some elements of the illness cannot be altered, or some of the difficulties your relative faces may not be things they can change, there is still plenty they can do to build up strength to deal with their situation. Changes can be made to lifestyle that will reduce risks in the future and help your relative adapt to new circumstances. For example, it can be helpful to:

■ *recognise that older people can become depressed fairly easily, and there is often an obvious cause;*

■ *look at the social side of their life, and put into place some interesting activities to give pleasure and prevent loneliness;*

■ *make some changes to diet and exercise routines, to help strengthen a body that might have been neglected in the course of the illness;*

■ *find ways of managing stress and coping with pressure during this anxious time. Chapter 8 suggests a range of methods – you could read it now if anxiety is a problem.*

The thought of making lifestyle changes may be daunting, so this chapter starts by offering some tips about making adjustments in general. None of the suggestions involve major changes, and not all the suggested changes will apply to the person you care for, so pick out the information that is relevant.

Janet has been caring for a relative with depression

'I can cope better if I am busy so I felt less frustrated when the doctor gave me a list of things to go away and do. I went to the library and found some information and made some changes to our routine.'

Harry is a general practitioner

'I always reassure my patients and their relatives that there is much they can do to help themselves. I find relatives always adjust better if they are allowed to take an active part in the care and treatment, however small.'

Moving forward from depression

Once your relative is feeling more stable, the time has come to look forward and think about staying well. However, this is not a process that can be rushed – you will need to take each step at a pace that suits your relative's individual pattern of progress. Avoid statements beginning 'When you are better', because a person who is recovering from depression might have only the most fragile belief in their own recovery. They are likely to find it difficult to think any distance ahead.

As the primary carer, you will have an important part to play in helping your relative to move forward in both a practical and an emotional sense. For example, you can encourage them to continue taking their medication for as long as the doctor advises.

Accompany them to any medical appointments if they would like your support, and plan the occasional social outing to help reduce loneliness and show them that life can still be enjoyed.

Dealing with any mental health illness is a difficult business, and you may well fear that the situation might get worse whatever the health professionals have told you. It is possible your relative's depression might return so monitor their mood discreetly, without making a big issue of how they feel. Be reassured that if treatments have worked in the past they will do so again, and assure your relative that feeling depressed is not a sign of failure or a symptom of old age. Keep in touch with the doctor or community psychiatric nurse, follow their advice and you and your relative will soon slip into a more relaxed pattern of life.

Making changes

A change in circumstances is always triggered by some event, no matter how insignificant. If you think about major changes in the past, something happened that set you off on a new course of action. Sometimes the event is outside your control, and you feel unsettled until you have come to terms with the new situation.

The illness of a relative you care about is an event that will trigger change. It is important you both spend time talking about how this situation has affected your lives. Think about how things were before the depression started (perhaps before a bereavement). Let relatives and friends offer support and don't try to block out memories of the illness because you won't be able to plan for the future while you still feel upset about what has happened. Allow time to grieve for the past – it is quite normal to want to do this when a traumatic event has occurred. When you feel ready, start putting changes into action. Your plans might centre on a range of issues such as financial arrangements, short and long term health, living accommodation and other practical matters. These all need careful thought.

> ### Janet
>
> 'I will always remember the community psychiatric nurse saying to me, "Understanding makes coping easier". She was right.'

If you or your relative are having difficulty accepting that change is taking place, it might help to talk about what is holding you up. Sometimes problems are larger in the mind than they are in reality. It's better if you can face problems squarely. Otherwise, although you think that you have dealt with all the worries, they merely spring up again in another guise. Rather than being resolved, they continue to dominate your thoughts. The change process can be very slow, so don't rush into a false sense of acceptance. As you sort out your affairs, bit by bit, the nightmare of dealing with huge changes will feel less of a burden.

In a quiet moment think about this list:

- **Do** look forward.
- **Do** make a list of the good things in life – however trivial they may seem.
- **Do** talk to someone about difficult decisions.
- **Do** accept that life moves forward.
- **Do** acknowledge your own feelings.
- **Do** try to find someone to talk through your feelings if you need to.
- **Do** remember help is available.
- **Don't** rush yourselves.
- **Don't** bottle up feelings.
- **Don't** feel guilty.
- **Don't** try to place blame.
- **Don't** look over your shoulder, hankering for a 'better' past.

General health care

Although many aspects of health, such as family history, are fixed, it is never too late to make changes for the better or to make the best of your current state of health. A good place to start is by taking a look at your everyday lifestyle.

Diet

Gillian is a dietitian

'The word "diet" usually conjures up images of sparse portions and grumbling hunger pangs. However, in this context, the word "diet" means "what your relative eats" rather than "how they can lose weight"! It is never too late to listen to general advice about sensible eating and there are specific diets to help them improve poor appetite and gain energy.'

Diet is an important factor in any health programme. Your relative may have become overweight or they may have been eating poorly – either type of eating behaviour can be affected by depression. Menus can be designed to build up strength or reduce calories, depending on what dietary regime is required. A review of what your relative eats could be one of the first changes you help them make, because adjusting the diet is a relatively easy step to take.

Having a good diet is one of the most important self-help recommendations from the charity Depression Alliance because the link between poor diet and depression is very strong. Dietary advice and a selection of leaflets should be readily available from the practice nurse at the local health centre or doctor's surgery. Patients taking antidepressants can eat a normal diet, unless they have been prescribed monamine oxidase inhibitors (MAOIs) because of the dangers associated with too much tyramine (see below). However, if your relative is experiencing any difficulties or if you feel you need specific advice, ask their doctor if they can be referred to a dietitian.

Some people inherit a tendency to be a certain shape and others gain or lose weight more readily than the next person. In basic terms, anyone who eats more, or fewer, calories than they burn up will usually go up or down in weight. The simple rules for controlling weight are, eat foods that are energy-rich to put on weight or foods that are calorie-reduced to lose weight. When helping your relative to cut back or increase their calories, it is important to keep an eye on the nutritional content of the diet and not reduce their intake of valuable vitamins and minerals. If your relative has a 'picky' appetite, select foods that give a good value per calorie. For example, chocolate is one of the first things that overweight people avoid but it is a useful source of iron, fat and calories, in an easily digestible form, if your relative is eating very little.

Amanda is a dietitian

'The good news is that a lot of benefit can be gained by making minor changes. It is important that your relative continues to enjoy food so don't make dramatic changes overnight – introduce new foods and cooking methods gradually and buy a variety of foods so that a healthy balance is maintained.'

Eating problems

People who are depressed may lose weight because they stop eating properly. If this is affecting your relative, check the list below to identify the reasons why they might be struggling to regain an interest in food. For example, are they:

- too tired to eat;
- too listless to feed themselves;
- suffering from a dry mouth (one of the side effects of taking antidepressants);
- finding their dentures no longer fit properly;
- suffering from indigestion after eating;
- constipated (another side effect of taking antidepressants);
- finding their food tastes unpleasant or dull.

Side effects of MAOIs (monoamine oxidase inhibitors)

These drugs can cause serious problems because they prevent the breakdown (digestion) of 'tyramine', a substance already present in the body as well as being found in a wide range of foods and over-the-counter medicines. A build up of tyramine in the blood causes a dangerous increase in blood pressure level which might induce a stroke. The first noticeable symptom is likely to be a throbbing headache. All foods and medicines containing tyramine must be excluded from the diet while a person is taking MAOIs, and for at least 14 days after finishing treatment with these drugs. The tyramine-rich foods to avoid include most cheeses, extracts of meat and yeast (Marmite, Oxo, Bovril etc), smoked or pickled fish, hung poultry and game, many wines and some beers. The labels on any drugs bought without a prescription should always be checked, especially cough medicines and laxatives. The problems caused by this group of drugs is sufficiently life-threatening to mean that all patients who are prescribed MAOIs are given a treatment card stating clearly which foods can and cannot be eaten. Understandably, these restrictions make the drug very unpopular, so it is not often prescribed now. If you or your relative are unsure about the dangers of taking MAOIs, do speak to a doctor or psychiatric nurse for advice.

Finding solutions

For general self-help and pick-me-up tips you could try the following suggestions:

- ask your relative what foods would trigger their taste-buds as small amount of 'snack' type food may be better than a 'proper' meal;
- provide smaller meals on a small plate to avoid the overwhelming sight of a normal-sized helping;
- let your relative eat on request, when they feel peckish;
- pick meals with interest and nutritional value, attractively presented;
- offer finger foods that can be picked at and put down (eg snack bars);
- keep food light – eating stodgy, hard-to-chew food saps energy quickly;
- ensure food is moist as this will be easier to eat than dry food;
- lubricate a dry mouth with flavoured ice-cubes or chunks of pineapple;

■ liquidise foods into easy-to-swallow drinks using milk or fruit juice as fluid;

■ keep the freezer well stocked with a choice of refreshing ice-creams;

■ try all-in-one meal drinks and use these as a drink after or instead of a meal (some makes are available on prescription);

■ avoid rich, spicy food if this causes indigestion; conversely if your relative's sense of taste is reduced try 'pepping up' taste-buds with strongly flavoured foods;

■ offer a straw if the mouth is sore or if it is easier to drink lying down;

■ offer a glass of sherry as an aperitif (see alcohol section below);

■ resist hassling your relative if they lose interest in food – a relaxed, 'no-problem' atmosphere is more likely to succeed;

■ offer a little help – cut food into manageable-sized portions or offer to feed your relative if they tire very easily;

■ sit with them for a bit and share a quiet meal – it's a good time to catch up on family news – and let them eat while you talk;

■ increase the proportion of fibre-rich/high residue foods if constipation is a problem due to the side effects of antidepressants and speak to your doctor, a pharmacist or nurse about taking gentle laxatives;

■ increase the proportion of foods that bind the stools (reduced fibre/low residue foods) if diarrhoea is causing discomfort – and seek advice.

Build-up diet

This way of eating is devised to help people maintain or build up their weight. It involves introducing into the diet foods that are high in energy and protein, with the emphasis on richness and increased calories. Many older people experience eating problems and everyone needs a certain level of energy to maintain their body mass, even if they are very inactive. A diet that is advised for someone who is losing weight, or to help increase weight, is designed especially for that purpose. It is not recommended long term for people who are eating well.

Choose a selection of foods regularly from the following lists when preparing meals, to help increase calories.

- **High energy foods** Bread, pasta, cereals, cake, sweet biscuits, and glucose sweets.
- **High protein foods** Meat, poultry, fish, beans, lentils, eggs, milk and cheese – but to reduce the risk of infection cook eggs well and avoid dairy products made from unpasteurised milk.
- **Rich fatty foods** Oils, butter, margarine, fatty meats and oily fish, full-fat dairy products (eg fresh cream), nuts and mayonnaise. Look for labels that state 'whole milk' and 'full-fat' rather than products that claim to be low-fat or 'light'.
- **Vitamins and minerals** While vitamins and minerals are contained in most foods, some of the best sources are raw or lightly cooked fruit and vegetables with the skins intact.

If your relative is frail and has lost weight use subtle ways to introduce extra goodness, without adding too much bulk. For example:

- Add extra milk or cream to soups, puddings, custard, mashed potato, breakfast cereals and drinks in the form of fortified milk foods (available from pharmacies), evaporated or condensed milk or dried milk powder and use milk when the recipe states water.
- Add extra lentils, split peas, beans or egg noodles to meat stews and casseroles.
- Put a spoonful of real cream, rich ice-cream or condensed milk on to puddings.
- Use extra honey or syrup on breakfast cereals or porridge (made with milk or single cream).
- Keep a selection of nibbles, such as peanuts, crisps and dried fruits in handy dishes about the house.
- Spread butter, margarine and mayonnaise more thickly, and add to mashed potato and vegetables.

Alcohol

In general, the main message from doctors and scientists suggests that, for the majority of people, alcohol taken in small amounts may be beneficial and does no obvious harm. It is also acknowledged that for a small proportion of the population, alcohol can have unpleasant effects and studies have made links between alcohol and depression. It is unclear which comes first, however. Do bouts of heavy drinking cause depression, or do people who are depressed turn to alcohol? It seems likely that those depressed people who overuse alcohol have an initial predisposition to depression. They may then start to drink excessively for several reasons. Alcohol has the ability to release the self-discipline that controls inhibition, and this feeling of 'letting go' might encourage depressed people to drink too much in the mistaken belief that it will relieve their mood, as in the expression 'drowning your sorrows'. Some people also believe that alcohol gives courage and the energy to cope with life. Unfortunately, any relief given by alcohol soon wears off. The feelings of depression then appear worse, and the inclination is likely to be to increase alcohol consumption. Doctors have reported that, when questioned about alcohol intake, depressed people tend to under-estimate their drinking habits by as much as 50 per cent. In the general population, excessive drinking is strongly linked to many causes of illness and death including cancer, liver disease, strokes, and accidental death.

In the face of evidence from many studies around the world, the most sensible advice is that alcohol should be drunk in moderation only. For the majority of people who are not suffering from depression, the recommended weekly amount is a maximum of 20 standard drinks for men. Women, who are less able to metabolise alcohol because they have a smaller liver, are advised to drink no more than 14 standard measures. Everyone is advised to restrict their drinking by taking at least 2–3 alcohol-free days each week to give their bodies a rest. It is also important to be aware that alcoholic drinks vary in potency, and that drinks poured at home tend to be larger than standard pub measures.

For people suffering from depression, the advice leans much more towards exercising caution and it is usually recommended that people taking antidepressants avoid alcohol completely, as they increase its effect. However, each patient should be assessed individually.

If your relative enjoys a drink and there is no evidence of alcohol abuse, the indications are that an occasional drink may be both pleasurable and beneficial. Do not encourage them to drink without their doctor's permission however, and aim to stay well below the recommended levels for the general population. If you have any concerns about the amount of alcohol your relative is drinking, approach the subject sensitively and try to work out between you how you might deal with the problem. Some tips include:

- helping your relative to avoid the temptation of using alcohol as a mood booster;
- advising them to sip drinks slowly to make each glass last longer;
- avoiding undiluted spirits or drinking on an empty stomach;
- offering non-alcoholic wines or beers, and exploring the wide range of soft drinks now available;
- suggesting that they seek help if the situation is becoming a problem.

For more *i*nformation

ⓘ Alcohol Concern offers information in the form of factsheets, leaflets and a journal but not direct advice (see page 202).

ⓘ Drinkline: providing confidential information, help and advice about drinking to anyone, including people worried about someone else's drinking (see page 208).

Smoking

People who have a mental illness are twice as likely to smoke cigarettes as those who don't. This habit puts them at greater risk of serious illness such as heart disease and lung cancer, and in some cases can interfere with the effectiveness of medications prescribed to treat their depression. Smoking is often used (wrongly) as a form of 'self-medication' because nicotine can have a powerful effect on mood. Some people with depression are less able to motivate themselves to quit although some antidepressants have been found to help. There is even some evidence to suggest that certain mental illnesses may be triggered or exacerbated by smoking.

It is a myth that smoking may not be harmful. The proven evidence from a large number scientific studies show that all forms of smoking (cigarettes, cigars and pipes) damage health. The facts about smoking-related illnesses make for sober reading. Smoking is the biggest avoidable cause of premature death and ill health; the earlier a person starts to smoke the greater their likelihood of developing smoking-related diseases.

Vijay, a general practitioner

'It's never too late to feel the benefits of giving up, and it's one of the most effective changes that anyone can make to improve their health. However, most GPs would not encourage a patient to give up smoking until their depression had lifted.'

Most people do understand that smoking is bad for their health, especially if a family member has developed a tobacco-related disease. If your relative smokes, they may have been told to give up. But the problem often lies, not in the acceptance that cigarette smoke is the culprit, but in the ability to actually stop. Quitting smoking is not an easy thing to do as long-term smokers are usually addicted to nicotine and may suffer severe withdrawal symptoms. It can be particularly difficult during a bout of depression when stress levels are increased by boredom, fears about their illness and anxiety about the future. If your relative's desire to smoke is very strong, attempting to give up while they are depressed may not be realistic. Be ready to offer encouragement when they are over the worst of the illness.

Tips to stop smoking

- Listen to your relative and try not to criticise any lapses. Be sympathetic but firm.
- However irritable they become, don't suggest they start smoking again.
- Change routines so that old habits don't make it easy to light up. Identify times and places that make your relative particularly

vulnerable to temptation, and alter behaviour if necessary. For example, suggest they sit in a different chair, drink tea instead of coffee and change routines after a meal – as all of these may be associated with a previous smoking habit.

■ Offer plenty to drink as ex-smokers need to flush the chemicals well out of their system. Fruit juice is particularly good as vitamin C helps to rid the body of nicotine.

■ Suggest different forms of entertainment to help combat boredom, particularly activities which involve using the hands.

■ Offer plenty of praise and support, but don't overdo the sympathy. Some sensitive people may prefer not to be reminded. Ask your relative which approach would work best for them.

■ Suggest that your relative tells people they need to give up for health reasons. That way family and friends won't smoke in their presence and, hopefully, won't tease them for their efforts.

■ Talk about the benefits of giving up. For example, after a few days the sense of taste and smell begin to return; after a few weeks the lungs are cleaner and breathing becomes easier; and after a year the risk of a heart attack is reduced by 50 per cent.

■ Highlight the money that is being saved, and think of ways you can use it to treat yourselves!

For more *i*nformation

i Talk to other ex-smokers or telephone the freephone helpline run by an independent charity *Quitline* (0800 002 200) that provides confidential and practical advice for people wanting to give up smoking.

i NHS Smoking Helpline 0800 169 0 169 offers similar help and support to give up all forms of smoking.

Exercise

Exercise is good news for everyone, even for people who are not particularly mobile. Whatever the level of physical activity a person undertakes, it must be tempered to suit their capabilities. Information in a book can only be written in a general way, so before you encourage your relative to take any form of exercise, they must check with their doctor first and be sure they understand what is suitable for them. As a carer, you can help your relative plan an exercise programme sensibly, perhaps with advice from a physio-therapist or occupational therapist who is skilled in rehabilitation. Not all exercise need be strenuous, and no one would suggest your relative take up vigorous sports. Start gently with a mild physical activity and consider joining in yourself – shared activity is much more pleasurable than exercising in isolation.

Mark is a leisure centre manager

'It is never too late to derive some benefit from exercise, the advantages are well proven. Exercise helps improves physical strength, mobility and mental well-being. It's very good for reducing stress as it boosts the hormones which produce feelings of happiness and the movement gently relaxes muscle tension. Muscles work more smoothly, with less effort, if they are made to work regularly. The Health Development Agency recommend exercise that boosts the three S's – strength, suppleness and stamina – all within moderation.'

Exercising safely

Whichever activity your relative chooses, it is important to be aware of a few safety rules, even after they have their doctor's approval:

- Start exercising gradually and build up exertion levels at a rate that feels comfortable. No-one should behave as if they are training for the Olympics.
- Don't exercise for at least two hours after a meal as the digestive system places an automatic demand on the blood supply to digest the food.
- Wear clothes that are loose and comfortable and shoes or trainers that provide adequate support.
- Never rush straight into the most strenuous part of the activity. Start and stop at a gentle pace to allow muscles to warm up and cool down before and after exercise.

- Drink plenty of fluids, but not alcohol as this increases dehydration.
- Stop immediately if there are any signs of breathlessness, chest pains or feeling unwell in any way. If exercise causes problems, however minor, it would be wise to inform the doctor before continuing with the programme.

John is a physiotherapist

'When starting to exercise after an illness such as depression, look at activities that get the body moving gently. Choose sports that are pleasurable not games that are stressful and competitive. Start off cautiously because too great an effort may reduce enthusiasm. Muscles that have been inactive need to stretch gently so "start and finish slowly" is the simple rule that can be applied to all the activities listed below.'

Ringing the changes

The following activities are classed as leisure hobbies rather than exercises for fitness fanatics; some can be done alone, some need a partner. If your relative would like to join a club, look in the local *Yellow Pages* or ask for details at the library.

- **Walking** This is a good choice if you have both been inactive as it boosts stamina and allows fitness to build up at a steady rate. Walking needs no special equipment, it is free, relaxing and pleasurable if shared with a companion. If your relative has become very debilitated by inactivity they must start very gently, perhaps with regular short walks gradually increasing the pace and distance over a few weeks.
- **Swimming** Another good exercise for people of all ages, swimming combines the three S's – stamina, strength and suppleness. It is often described as the ideal activity and can be a great stress reducer. Swimming is especially good for people who are overweight or have joint or back problems as the water supports the body. Most people live within reasonable distance of a swimming pool and the charges are often reduced for certain categories of people.

- **Cycling** This is another good exercise for improving on the three S's. It is recommended for people who are overweight and helps reduce stress as well as being pleasurable. Cycling in the fresh air is the best choice but an indoor cycle machine provides an alternative way to 'get pedalling'.
- **Golf** Golf is a great energiser. It helps build up stamina and strength, provides fresh air and an opportunity to make new friends. Start off gently with a few holes and stop to enjoy the company and scenery.
- **Gardening** This is a wonderfully relaxing way to combine exercise with fresh air and do lots of bending and stretching. Recent research into horticultural therapy has shown it to be very beneficial for people affected by depression.
- **Bowling** Your relative may like to join a club to get the best advantage from indoor and grass bowls and try the ten pin variety with younger family members for some challenging play. All forms of bowling are excellent for suppleness and relaxation.
- **Badminton** This enjoyable game suits all ages as long as partners of similar ability are matched. At club level it can be quite a vigorous sport, so encourage your relative to build up skills at a pace that is comfortable and check with the doctor before starting this type of exercise.
- **Exercise and dance classes** These are readily available in most areas. Ask at a leisure centre about classes to suit your relative's age and ability level. Both types of exercise are good for stamina, strength and suppleness. Tea dances are especially relaxing and enjoyable.
- **Yoga** Good for suppleness and strengthening body muscles, yoga is an excellent form of exercise. It will help you or your relative to control movements and breathing, and will encourage muscle relaxation.

Leg cramps

Even small increases in exercise may cause leg cramps for some people, particularly if it is after a long period of inactivity. Your relative's doctor will advise about taking exercise if leg cramps are painful.

For more *i*nformation

i For details of a local adult sport and leisure activity classes contact the Community Education department at your local education authority, or private leisure centres.

i The Sports Council provides general information about all sports (see page 216).

i EXTEND provides recreational movement to music for older and less able people. EXTEND is active in many parts of the UK and trained teachers provide one-to-one sessions for those who require specialised exercise (see page 209).

Sleeping well

Depression, tension and stress are at the heart of many sleep problems, causing early waking or difficulty dropping off as thoughts race around the brain. If stress is making you or your relative sleep badly, don't rush for medication. Instead, try practising the relaxation techniques described in Chapter 8. You also need to be aware that older people naturally take longer to fall asleep, are more likely to wake during the night and tend to wake earlier in the morning. However, if sleep disturbance continues to be a problem do encourage your relative to discuss this with their doctor.

Tips to help settle at night

The following suggestions may be helpful:

■ go to bed at a regular time, with a regular routine;
■ make everything as cosy as possible, with a warm room and comfortable bed;
■ don't eat a rich, heavy meal late in the day;
■ avoid stimulating drinks that contain alcohol or caffeine later in the day and choose a milky drink at bedtime;
■ cut back on evening fluids if a full bladder is the cause of waking;

- read or listen to the radio until the mind feels naturally sleepy;
- if waking in the night is a problem do something to break the fidgety mood – rather than lie tossing and turning, get up and watch some television and repeat the milky drink with a biscuit;
- take regular exercise to tire the body, but not too late in the day as strenuous exercise releases hormones that are stimulating;
- rest and cat-nap during the day but resist having too long a sleep as this simply reduces the amount needed at night. (A 'power nap' of no more than 10 minutes can be rejuvenating.)

Dealing with extreme tiredness

Fatigue is more than just being 'tired', it is feeling completely exhausted most of the time. Extreme tiredness is a problem that many depressed people experience at some stage. Symptoms of fatigue may interfere with the most basic activities such as climbing stairs, brushing teeth and eating food. Shortness of breath is common and people with severe tiredness find it too arduous to carry on a conversation, concentrate to read or even watch the television. If your relative is experiencing sleep deprivation to the extent that they suffering this degree of fatigue, their doctor may arrange for them to have an Electro-encephalogram (EEG). In this harmless test, electrodes are attached to the scalp to measure electrical wave activity in the brain. A special machine records any abnormalities in the EEG waves produced while the person is asleep.

Judy is a community psychiatric nurse

'Fatigue is made worse by a combination of factors related to illness and treatments – poor appetite, lack of sleep, anxiety, and anaemia may all contribute. Trying to battle against extreme weariness increases debility, so persuade your relative that for a while it may be easier to give in and let others take over the major tasks of shopping, laundry and household chores. Help your relative to plan their day so that they can achieve the things that are most important to them, with lots of rest periods in between.'

Safety

Taking antidepressant tablets might make your relative drowsy, but this should wear off. If insomnia is a problem, however, antidepressants can be prescribed in such a way as to target sleep patterns. Observe your relative's habits at other times of the day and if they show signs of drowsiness be aware of the hazards and take some precautions to ensure their safety, especially with fires, hot drinks and cigarettes. If they are still driving a car, it may be wise to ask the doctor for advice. On the one hand getting out and about encourages independence and helps to tackle the depression but this must be balanced against the risk to themselves and other road users.

Relationships

People who have known each other and/or lived together for a period of time often become very close when one partner is ill, offering each other tremendous support through the bad moments and sharing joy and relief when times are good. However, carers do sometimes feel resentful because the ill person gets all the attention and they are left coping with the practical and emotional difficulties. If you have felt left out of the picture it may help to talk to a counsellor (see page 32). This will also help you to keep a balance in your mind between what is necessary now for your relative and the life to which you will return in the longer term.

Joseph is a counsellor

'Helping a friend or relative who is affected by depression can provide the opportunity to strengthen a relationship. It can also be frustrating and affect your health.'

Adam is a psychologist

'People can express love for each other in many ways and being a carer as well as a partner is one clear example. But, however close you are to your partner, making the adjustment from a caring relationship back (or forward) into a sexual relationship maybe a major step. A professional person will not be embarrassed to discuss the matter and will be able to reassure you both; usually, there are few reasons to hinder a sexual relationship, if this is what you both want.'

It is usual for sexual interest to diminish during a period of depression and this lack of desire may be accentuated by antidepressant medication. The most common problems are:

- lowered arousal;
- reduced performance;
- feeling less pleasure;
- inability to reach orgasm;
- difficulty in creating or maintaining an erection in men;
- premature ejaculation or difficulty ejaculating in men.

If sexual relationships have suffered between you (the carer) and your partner, and you wish to continue to be sexually active, there are many ways that pleasure can be achieved other than by direct sexual intercourse. For example, caressing someone gently is a non-threatening way to give and receive comfort. Be guided by your partner's mood and be careful about expressing negative feelings. A person who is struggling to cope with their own fragile emotions may not be able to handle yours as well. Be flexible about the time of day that you explore sexual pleasure – night time, after a tiring day may not be best time to choose. If problems persist after a reasonable time period, ask for advice from your specialist, GP or psychiatric nurse. They will either be able to advise you or help you to get more specialist advice if this would be useful. The early signals that indicate the return of sexual feelings usually mean the depression is lifting.

Impotence

Vijay is a general practitioner

'Male and female impotence may be a temporary problem following some types of treatment. If impotence is affecting your relative do encourage him or her to seek help from a doctor as a range of treatments are available. A change of drugs or simple relaxation therapy may be all that is needed to improve the situation.'

In the case of male impotence, the doctor may ask if the man can achieve a morning erection as this information will help to define whether the cause is physical rather than due to over-anxiety. For example, the effects of antidepressant drugs might be reducing the ability to have or sustain an erection, also a poor blood supply to the penis can affect the quality of an erection, particularly in an older man. For women, impotence may be signalled by a strong wish not to be bothered by sexual advances, often called extreme 'frigidity', which can lead to failure to allow vaginal penetration (vaginissmus). Quite a high proportion of women attending genito-urinary clinics describe sexual dysfunction and admit to tolerating painful intercourse. This condition may be brought about by their depression, but worrying about a problem like this could make the depression worse. If sexual intercourse remains a problem it may be helpful if both partners can be patient with foreplay. In addition, they may find it helpful to use plenty of lubrication as this eases any discomfort which might distract either one of them.

For more *i*nformation

ℹ️ Association to Aid the Sexual and Personal Relationships of the Disabled (see address on page 203).

Relieving boredom

Suzanne

'Jim was used to being busy and he did find it strange to have no energy and poor concentration. I bought a bonsai kit which helped to reduce his boredom but did not need long spells of concentration.'

When concentration is at a low ebb, don't expect too much from your relative. It is well recognised that people who are depressed lose their powers of attention and this makes activities like chess and heavy reading virtually impossible. There are many ways to lift the spirit and relieve boredom without being too demanding. A gentle walk in the garden or along the pavement for a few minutes may be sufficient. Try talking about childhood times, looking at photograph albums, glancing at a magazine or listening to very gentle music. Ask your relative about the type of activities and company they think they would – or would not – enjoy. In the early days, interaction with other people may be nerve racking so do not arrange social events that will cause distress. As your relative's health improves, try to get out of the house as soon as it is practicable to get a change of scene and overcome fears about leaving a safe place. Enlist the help of family and friends for all manner of support – from shoppers and drivers to companions and listeners. Try to gauge how your relative feels as you may need to act in a 'gatekeeping' role if offers of help are overwhelming.

Delia

'I found it very frightening to watch my mother just sitting in the chair and staring into space. I tried to chat about her favourite TV soap stars but she hadn't even watched the programme.'

Suzanne and Jim

'We joined a Spanish class at the local college when Jim felt much better. He felt confident to go out and meet people and we promised ourselves a holiday as a future goal.'

As your relative gains confidence, suggest some active entertainment as well as the more passive type, but set achievable goals to promote their motivation. A trip to an art gallery or an afternoon cinema programme may be just what is needed to trigger mental and social stimulation and boost confidence. The public library is the best source of information: most branches carry a wide range of details about local services, with some specialist facilities targeted at carers. As well as books of all sorts, look out for:

- lists of clubs and hobby groups;
- audio and video tapes;
- mobile and doorstep library services for home delivery of books and tapes to people who experience significant difficulty getting to a library because of illness, disability or caring responsibilities;
- 'Talking News' style services providing a range of interesting items via postal tapes – usually for visually impaired people but often extended to people with other disabilities;
- 'befriending' schemes where volunteers come to the house to chat or play games with people who are temporarily or permanently housebound;
- branches of University of the Third Age (U3A) that offer a vast range of day time study and recreational classes for people who are older and wish to keep their minds stimulated (see address on page 217).

Volunteering

Sheila is a volunteer centre manager

'Volunteering is an excellent way to get yourself back into the community after an illness. Voluntary sector organisations treat people with care, so don't be worried about telling them you are recovering from depression. Many of the new volunteers who come to the centre for information are nervous at first but we soon put them at ease.'

Doing some voluntary work for a local charity is an excellent way to boost the morale. Volunteering is definitely a two way process where a volunteer gives their time to help a group or individual person in need and in return they can meet new people, undertake an interesting activity and take pleasure in being useful. Age or mental health illnesses are rarely a barrier. The range of volunteering opportunities available in most areas is very comprehensive. Your relative could choose to befriend an older person, listen to children reading in school, help with fundraising activities, work in a charity shop or do some environmental work. Most areas have a centre where potential volunteers can go along for a chat about how they can become involved. Information is readily available and there shouldn't be any pressure to join a group before one feels ready. Look in the telephone directory for Volunteer Bureau/Centre/Agency, contact the local library or the national office for Volunteer Agencies (Volunteer Development England) and ask for a local address (see page 218).

Transport and mobility

As recovery continues your relative may want to venture further from home, perhaps for a shopping trip or a hospital appointment. But travel may be a problem if driving is restricted. Look out for transport schemes for older and disabled people, available in most areas and run by local authorities and voluntary organisations. The journey is free or subsidised, depending on personal circumstances and carers are welcome as escorts. Fares to hospital can be reimbursed for certain categories of people (see page 157).

The main schemes to help people with transport are listed below:

- **Dial-a-Ride and Community Transport Schemes** These provide door to door services for shopping or similar outings for people who cannot use public transport (see pages 206–207).
- **Hospital Car Schemes** Such schemes are usually run by the ambulance service and arranged through GPs' surgeries. They are available only for people who have a medical condition and cannot get to the hospital independently. One companion is usually allowed.
- **The Blue Badge Scheme** This provides a national arrangement of parking concessions for people with severe walking difficulties who travel as drivers or passengers. Badge holders are exempted from certain parking restrictions – including free parking at on-street parking meters and for up to two hours on single and double yellow lines in England and Wales. Badges are issued for a three-year period through social services departments. Check local rules carefully as some London Boroughs do not offer free parking arrangements.
- **Motability** This charity was set up to help those disabled people who want to spend the mobility component of their Disability Living Allowance or War Pensioner's Mobility Supplement on a car or wheelchair. Vehicles may be purchased or leased and help may be available with the cost of special adaptations. A relative, friend or carer may apply and drive on behalf of a disabled person (see page 212).
- **Concessionary rail fares** All train operators have a railcard that offers concessionary fares to disabled people, giving up to one third off a range of rail tickets. An application form and booklet called *Rail Travel for Disabled Passengers* can be found at most stations or from the Disabled Persons Railcard Office (see page 208). All rail operators give extra help to older or disabled travellers, particularly if they have advanced notice.
- **Shopmobility** Shopmobility schemes provide free wheelchair or scooter loan services in many town centres for anyone with

a mobility problem. Users can usually park free or be met at the bus station or taxi rank by prior arrangement. An escort service is often available for people who are visually impaired or wheelchair users.

- **Taxicard** This and other similar services provide subsidised taxi fares. They are run by many local authorities for permanently disabled people who are unable to use public transport. One passenger may accompany the cardholder. Ask at your town hall.

- **Tripscope** Tripscope offers a free nationwide travel and transport information and advice service for older and disabled people (see page 216). Tripscope will help with planning a journey, but it is not a travel agency so cannot make bookings.

- **The Community Transport Association** This association has services to benefit providers of transport for people with mobility problems (see page 206).

- **The Disability Living Allowance Unit** Part of the Department of Work and Pensions (see page 217 under 'Vehicle Excise Duty'), this unit gives information about exemption from road tax for vehicles used exclusively by or for disabled people receiving the higher rate of the mobility component of Disability Living Allowance (DLA) or War Pensioners' Mobility Supplement. You may claim on behalf of the person you look after by completing an application form from the Benefits Agency.

For more *i*nformation

ⓘ Age Concern Factsheet 26 *Travel information for older people*.

ⓘ Contact your local authority for more information about local schemes to help with transport.

Holidays

Jeanne

'We started off with a mini-break to build up our confidence. When that went OK we felt safe to book a longer holiday.'

Once your relative is feeling better you may all benefit from a holiday. The GP will advise you about when the time is right and explain the main aspects of your relative's health care, especially if you are going abroad. At the planning stage it would be wise to find out about the following points in case you need to make special arrangements for:

- taking drugs out of the country;
- insurance cover because your relative has an existing illness;
- dealing with the effects of heat and sunlight (or opt for somewhere with a cooler climate).

Holiday planning services that specifically deal with information for older or disabled people can be used, and this may reduce much of the load on you. The organisations listed below are selected from the many that provide help.

For more *i*nformation

i Age Concern Factsheet 4 *Holidays for older people.*

i Air Transport Users Council publishes a booklet *Care in the Air* for disabled passengers (see page 202).

i Holiday Care Service provides information and advice on holidays, travel facilities and respite care available for people with disabilities, those on low income and people with special needs. A reservation helpline and holiday insurance information for disabled people are available (see page 210).

i RADAR (Royal Association for Disability and Rehabilitation) provides information about many aspects of disability, including accessible destinations for holidays (see page 214).

i Special Families Home Swap Register produces a quarterly register to enable physically disabled people to swap their home for breaks elsewhere in the country. The homes listed are suitably equipped to accommodate people with physical disabilities. A small fee is charged for registration but there are no other costs; accommodation is free.

i Winged Fellowship provides respite care and holidays for physically disabled people, with or without a partner, in purpose built holiday centres and on overseas and touring holidays. Trained staff and volunteers provide care (see page 218).

Maintaining the good times

When the depression has eased there are still a few things you can encourage your relative to do, to build on all your hard work and help to prevent a backward step.

■ Encourage your relative to continue taking the medication for as long as the doctor recommends. Stopping early is not a good move even if the symptoms are no longer noticeable and they feel fully recovered.

■ Continue to visit the therapist if a 'talking' therapy has been part of the treatment programme. The frequency of the appointments can be scaled down.

■ Continue any routines and techniques that have been useful. This can be likened to playing a musical instrument where failure to practice soon leads to reduced skills.

■ Build on the strengths that have been gained. You probably both have a better insight into how you think and feel, so use this self-knowledge to your advantage. At the first signs of impending depression step up the self-help techniques before it takes a hold.

■ Keep fit and active. Stimulation of both the mind and the body is a great way to help keep well in older age.

■ Above all don't get worried by the odd day where feelings seem low. It is absolutely normal for mood to fluctuate, and not a signal that should necessarily alarm you.

Sita and Sanjay

'Suffering a serious illness such as depression results in many changes – don't give in and feel sorry for yourself. OK, so it might return. But while you are feeling stronger, make use of the time and do some of the things that you've promised yourself for years.'

For more *i*nformation

ℹ️ Disabled Living Centres Council will tell you about the Centre nearest you, where you can see and try out aids and equipment (see page 208).

ℹ️ Disabled Living Foundation provides information and advice about all aspects of daily living for people with disability (see page 208).

ℹ️ *Family Doctor* booklets in a range of titles are available from pharmacies or chemist shops.

ℹ️ NHS Direct provides confidential health advice and information, 24 hours a day, seven days a week. The helplines are staffed by qualified nurses and health information advisors who can offer immediate medical advice and reassurance. Tel: 0845 4647.

Conclusion

This chapter has encouraged you to focus on some of the changes that are happening to you and your relative, and has offered some hints as to how you might move forward. Adjusting to new situations is never easy, especially if the event that triggered the change was both distressing and beyond your control. We all deal with problems more effectively if we feel that an element of choice is involved and we are able to exercise some control over the situation. With depression, it may feel that this is not the case. However, there are lots of ways that self-help can be practised and it is important to maintain a positive outlook. After a while unpleasant memories do fade, and you and your relative will be able to look ahead with greater confidence and perhaps benefit from changes in lifestyle. Whatever the long term future holds, you will be able to access services when your relative needs more care.

The next chapter gives advice on dealing with your relative if they are not so well and Chapter 8 provides an insight into causes of stress and offers some techniques to help you both cope while you adjust.

6 How to cope with failing health

However well you care for your relative, their general health may begin to fail because it is inevitable that the health of an older person will eventually deteriorate. Your personal philosophy for dealing with this situation is a private matter, and you may or may not choose to ask for support. But many of the practical difficulties will be the same for all carers. If your relative is also suffering from depression you are likely to experience additional problems.

This chapter provides useful information to help you make future plans. It may seem difficult, or even wrong, to start thinking about failing health before that time arises but many families say it is less stressful to make tentative decisions and plans while they are relatively calm. Talking about the forthcoming period is not morbid, it is a part of the process that helps you all come to terms with changing circumstances.

Caring for an ill person at home is a difficult undertaking which sets up a mixture of emotions. Carers experience tremendous reward coupled with extreme tiredness; they feel anxious and sad and frequently become frustrated at the inadequacies of the 'system'. Despite these hurdles it is possible to overcome the problems and many carers feel determined to provide quality care at home for as long as possible.

*There are no right or wrong decisions, nor are there
effortless ways of dealing with the position. Simply do the
best you can, and make use of the help that is available
when you feel you have reached that stage.*

Short and long term care

New and more experienced carers continually reach stages when
they need to break fresh ground – perhaps by taking on increased
responsibilities and seeking additional support. The first part of
this chapter helps you to assess the type of help you might need.
It then guides you through the maze of information about what services are available for older and disabled people (including those
with depression) and their carers, and how they and you can
access the health and social care systems. Later in the chapter,
basic material is offered to help you care for your relative as their
health worsens.

Do you need help?

Rhoda

'Until I talked to the community psychiatric nurse I never realised that
there were so many organisations that provide support. I would have
struggled on alone whereas the help has been tremendous.'

Look at the checklist below and if you answer 'yes' to any of the questions and would like further information, you can ask for help locally.
Ask at your surgery, health centre or social services department.

■ Have you just started to care for someone else whose health is
   failing?

■ Do you think the person you care for should have an assessment or re-assessment of their needs?

■ Do you want to talk to someone about how you feel and what you are entitled to receive?

■ Would you like to know more about respite care facilities?

■ Do you feel exhausted and close to breaking point?

■ Do you need help to move your relative safely – for either your sake or theirs?

■ Do you think extra equipment would help you to manage better?

■ Do you feel you have received a poor quality service or support from those providing care?

Judy is a community psychiatric nurse

'If you are unsure about any aspect of caring speak to your community nurse, initially, without having to see the GP. We know all about local services and can often refer you to many services directly.'

Even if you have been caring for a while, you may still be unfamiliar with the full range of services. Why not find out what is available before pressure builds up and you reach crisis point? Community nurses or social workers are often thought to be a last point of call, but they can give support and advice to carers long before the crisis stage is reached. The community nurse is one of the key people for accessing other services.

The assessment process, and how it can help you and your relative, is described in greater detail below. It is the entry point to all types of care and is open to anyone who feels they are in need of a support service. Getting extra help does not mean that you have failed or that you are receiving charity. Families can be surprised and overwhelmed by the speed of change and deterioration in the health of their relative. It is not wrong to make enquiries that show you are anticipating future need.

Being informed

Tanya is a carers' support worker

'Take a pen and paper with you to make notes when you visit the surgery or any other professional worker. Take your time – although GPs and nurses appear busy people they would not wish you to misunderstand because you are feeling nervous.'

Being informed is a major factor in maintaining control when you are dealing with difficult issues. Knowing what might be offered, even if you are a bit hazy, makes a basic starting point when you seek additional support. Don't try to remember everything you are told but do try to make a note of the key headings that services fall under. For example, your rights as a carer, domestic help, where you can obtain equipment. If your relative is terminally ill, help and support should be available immediately. Gathering information now could save time later and give you your peace of mind and when your energies will be needed elsewhere. Set up an information folder and keep a notebook if it will help organise your affairs.

Lesley is a general practitioner

'The surgery is often the first place to ask for help. Keep 'knocking on the door' if you feel frustrated about getting an answer – you sometimes need to make your GP understand what you want. GPs should be a signpost to other services and if you need a home visit tell the receptionist why.'

Local support services

Support for you as a carer and for your relative is available locally from a number of sources run by statutory, private and voluntary organisations. Most of these services can be accessed via the NHS or the social services departments, and your relative will be assessed as requiring 'nursing' care or 'personal' care. There may seem to be little difference in practical terms, and in reality the services try to work very closely together. However, it does make a difference to the way the need for care is assessed and how care is paid for. Changes in care provision brought about after a top-level inquiry has resulted in a National Service Framework which sets out standards of care for older people, whether they are being cared for at home, in a care home or in hospital. There are numerous procedures (and promises) governed by this Framework, which came into effect in April 2001. It includes a one-stop assessment process for health and social care, and new legislation that helps to ease the financial burden of long term care in a care home. It is not possible to outline all of the procedures here so carers are advised to ask for a fuller explanation, from the appropriate authority when they are making decisions about care requirements. Many agencies use contract workers but all care is regulated by the National Care Standards Commission under the Care Standards Act (England) 2000 and Regulations of Care (Scotland) 2001.

Charges

Charges for care homes vary according to the type of care provided. After October 2001, nursing care was made free in any setting in England and Wales. In Scotland, personal care (in addition to nursing care) became free after April 2000. If State financial help is not required, private homes are available without undergoing an assessment. However, even if your relative is willing and able to meet the full fees, it is still a good idea to ask for an assessment from social services to help you choose the right sort of home and ensure that all the options are clear. Up-to-date information can be obtained from social services customer relations department or similar office in the local authority; look for the telephone number under Social Services ('Social Work' in Scotland) or the Primary Care Trust or relevant Age Concern Factsheets.

Social services departments can charge recipients of services (but rarely carers) for many of their services, depending on personal circumstances. If a person requests services or accommodation through a local authority, the local authority concerned has a legal duty to carry out an assessment, using a set of eligibility criteria. This should determine whether, and at what level, care might be needed. The local authority must also then pay for meeting any necessary care costs, at the agreed level, after a means test. A means test is an assessment of a person's financial circumstances. The assessment looks at long term needs; however, there are provisions that allow authorities to make a reasonable charge for placements of less than five weeks.

After a needs assessment has been completed, the cost of any care services offered will be explained before a care plan is agreed. The rates that apply under the charging procedure are set nationally by central government and are subject to change. The needs assessment and the financial assessment are undertaken separately and the results should have no bearing on each other. People who are eligible for payment of nursing care, if they have continuing physical or mental healthcare needs, are assessed against a set of established criteria.

For more *i*nformation

ⓘ Age Concern Factsheet 10 *Local authority charging procedures for residential and nursing home care.*

Social services

Sara is a carers' support worker

'Carers are bombarded with information when they are desperate and least able to listen calmly – it is much better to take in small pieces of advice when it is most needed rather than try and remember everything at once.'

Local social services departments are the main agencies for co-ordinating the provision of community care services for older people. Not all people with depression will require direct services from a social services department, for some families such information will be helpful. In all areas close liaison takes place between community psychiatric and general nurses and social workers and care will be shared when necessary.

Social services assessments, care plans and eligibility criteria

Carers UK

'When carers have an assessment they get more services.'

Sara, carers' support worker

'Unfortunately services are reduced when budgets are tight. Carers must ask for a proper assessment, this is a legal right.'

Social services departments are responsible for providing a wide range of home, residential and day care services. This is provided direct through their own home care service, or purchased for your relative from voluntary or commercial organisations (sometimes called the independent sector). Unfortunately, demand for services is heavy and most departments have limited financial resources so they apply strict eligibility criteria (tests) to decide which services to provide. These assessments, in some form, apply generally throughout the UK, though there are some local variations. The example of assessment given below is typical, although the availability of individual services will differ from area to area.

The first stage of the **assessment** process is intended to gather basic information about the situation and the care needs. It will usually take place in an appropriate surrounding as a face-to-face meeting and time will be taken to answer your questions. However,

125

certain details may be discussed beforehand by telephone to establish the urgency of the situation. At the end of the assessment the care needs of your relative are clearly defined and, if no further help and advice is needed, an agreement is reached with your relative (provided they are mentally capable) and you about what those care needs are. For the purpose of assessment these fall into five basic categories:

- **physical safety**, eg the person has regular falls;
- **physical disability**, eg mobility, sight or hearing problems;
- **mental health**, eg severe depression leading to neglect;
- **loss of independent living skills**, eg inability to cook, wash or dress themselves;
- **social needs**, eg the person has become very isolated and lonely.

The assessor then decides the _level of need_ from low to very high risk.

Once it is decided that a person is eligible to receive services, discussions take place between everyone immediately involved to devise a care plan that best suits the needs of the family. The eligibility criteria continue to apply if your relative is already receiving services. The needs of you both will be re-assessed by means of a review and services may change as a result of this process. Again, everyone immediately concerned will be fully involved and informed of any decisions about future care. If you do not agree with the result of the assessment, you may appeal against it via the social services complaints procedure (a social worker or care manager will advise you about the process). Social services departments will investigate any complaint seriously and will suggest that you obtain independent advice. The local Citizens Advice Bureau may be able to advise you.

Home care (social services)

Help for adults with day to day living in their own homes includes:

- personal care (eg washing, toileting, going to bed);
- practical help (eg housework or shopping) although this type of help is more likely to be provided by a separate agency;

- help for carers who may be partners, relatives or friends (eg respite care);
- advice and equipment from an occupational therapist (eg commodes, bed raisers);
- help for people with specialist needs from specialist staff (eg those with hearing or sight loss, or physical disabilities).

Care assistants give personal care, such as washing and toileting, and do basic treatments. They are not trained nurses so do not carry out elaborate nursing procedures.

Since April 2002, the way charges are calculated for home care in Scotland differ slightly to that in England and Wales. Guidelines giving the appropriate charging structures are available locally.

Health care services (NHS)

Services from the NHS for people with health care needs include the provision of general and specialist care, loan of equipment, rehabilitation, respite health care and continuing NHS care (ie, care the NHS pays for in full). This latter point can mean that the NHS pays the full fees for agreed nursing care. The main decisions about what health services will be provided for people locally are taken by Primary Care Trusts, which also commission services from other NHS Trusts and the independent sector, to complement their own provision. You can get information about health services from your GP surgery or health centre, or from NHS Direct. NHS and social services staff should work closely with your GP to maintain continuity of care.

Local health services tend to fall into three categories:

- **acute health care**, given at NHS hospital trusts that offer specialist tests and treatments through inpatient and outpatient services;
- **community health care**, provided by NHS Primary Care Trusts that offer day to day care from a range of services, including

127

community psychiatric and general nursing, physiotherapy, occupational therapy and chiropody;

■ **tertiary health care**, provided by care homes.

Eligibility criteria for continuing NHS health care

Each NHS Trust sets its eligibility criteria for these services based on national guidelines. They must be published and should be available from the local NHS body. Your relative's health care needs will be assessed against these criteria. Some older patients may have longer-term care needs than younger patients. The 'eligibility' assessment process will be broached sensitively for patients with mental health problems. An NHS patient receiving treatment in hospital and requiring services after discharge, will be assessed before leaving hospital. If long-term, hospital-based care is not needed, social services and NHS professionals will work together to prepare a Care Plan (set of services) to be provided in their own home or a care home. The care given to each patient is overseen by one senior person who will work with a small team of staff to ensure consistent care. The name given to this key person may vary from area to area, but it is designed to fulfil the same purpose – the role of care 'manager'.

The views and wishes of the person and their family are taken into account. If they do not agree with the decision to discharge the patient from hospital they can ask an independent review panel to look at the decision. If this applies to you, the Patient Advice and Liaison Service (PALS) in England, the Community Health Councils in Wales, the Mental Health Commission in Northern Ireland, or the Health Council in Scotland can help you if you are unsure how to proceed. Your GP surgery or health centre should have contact details, which should also be in the local telephone directory.

Home care (NHS)

The Community Nursing Service operates throughout the country providing general and psychiatric nursing treatment and care for people who remain at home. Community psychiatric and general nurses are often based at GP surgeries and health centres; patients are usually referred by their GPs but anyone can contact a community nurse direct. If a care plan has already been set up following hospital discharge, the appropriate community nurse will call automatically. But if your relative has not been discharged recently and you feel you need help or advice, you may telephone for an assessment. Don't wait until you are desperate, particularly if the state of your relative's mental health is failing or they have become incontinent. Community nurses can provide a great deal of local information about resources and can put you in touch with other services and arrange equipment and items such as incontinence pads. Ask for a telephone number at your surgery or leave a message for the nurse.

Emily

'I felt so relieved when the community nurses came to us. I wanted my husband to stay at home so when he was getting weaker a nurse showed me how to move him around at regular hours and helped me sort out the right times for all his pills.'

For more *i*nformation

i Age Concern Factsheet 32 *Disability and ageing: your rights to social services.*

i Age Concern Factsheet 37 *Hospital discharge arrangements, and NHS continuing health care services.*

i Age Concern Factsheet 20 *NHS Continuing Care, free nursing care and intermediate care.*

i NHS Direct on 0845 4647, a 24-hour information and helpline available in England.

Pharmacists (chemists) and prescriptions

Pharmacists provide a number of services to the community and are a valuable source of information about medicines, 'over-the-counter' treatments (which don't need a prescription) and any minor health problems not serious enough to take to a surgery. Pharmacists will advise you to speak to the GP if they feel there is a need for medical treatment. Before you speak to a pharmacist, make a list of all medication your relative is taking, so that he or she can be sure that drugs will not interact with each other.

Pharmacists have particular responsibility for making up prescriptions for medicines or certain medical aids. You may take a prescription to any pharmacy but, for people living in rural areas, a dispensing service is available at surgeries and health centres if the nearest pharmacist/chemist shop is more than one mile away. Ask about the availability of this service if you are unsure. There is normally a charge for prescriptions, but certain groups of people qualify for free medication. These include people on income support, people over retirement age, and people with certain illnesses such as diabetes. Having depression does not automatically mean that your relative will be exempt.

Pharmacists can help in other ways, such as supplying and /or filling a 'Doset' box to help someone take the correct drug dose at the correct time of day and putting medicines in non child-proof containers if a person has difficulty opening standard caps. (See page 58 for advice on safety and medicines.)

Pre-payment certificates are available to help spread the cost for people who need regular medication but do not qualify for free prescriptions. Enquire about these or any other pharmacy-related details at your local pharmacy, chemist or GP surgery.

Voluntary services

There is a wide range of voluntary organisations providing services, self-help and support to carers at national and regional levels. Some voluntary organisations provide services that are broadly targeted – for example the advice and information available from Citizens Advice Bureaux – while others offer help with specific diseases such as depression. Services provided by the voluntary sector may carry charges to cover costs.

Many voluntary sector organisations are directly contracted by the NHS and social services to provide care locally. The services are professionally managed by well trained staff; day centres for older patients, transport schemes and meals on wheels are good examples. National charities dealing with depression offer support through telephone helplines, newsletters and self-help groups. Many also have local branches.

No two areas will offer identical services, so you will have to find out what you can expect to obtain in your part of the country. The two main signposting organisations for local voluntary sector services can be found in the telephone directory under Council for Voluntary Services (CVS) and Volunteer Bureau (or contact their national associations, see pages 212 and 218).

Specialist agencies

There are many organisations that work directly with and for people with mental health problems – too many to cover fully here. The larger charities offer materials and advice covering all aspects of treatments and some provide direct 'hands-on' care. The smaller charities tend to offer a specialist service. Many charities also fund, undertake and/or support research into mental ill health. For contact details of the main charities see the 'For more information' section at the end of Chapter 2. Ask at your GP surgery or health centre what is available in your local area. The full range of services, spread across several organisations, is very varied including:

■ written literature, eg leaflets, fact sheets, books, newsletters;
■ audio and visual tapes for people with impaired senses, and the provision of clear, pictorial information for all patients and carers;

- Internet access to website material, including texts similar to leaflets and fact sheets;
- helpline services that enable patients and carers to speak directly to a trained nurse or counsellor;
- access to urgent welfare items where there is a time delay or absence in statutory provision;
- training programmes for doctors and nurses to improve the care and treatment of mental health patients and to help professional workers be better informed so that they can promote a greater understanding among the public.

The key charities are listed alphabetically in the address section at the end of the book. Contact their national offices for direct information or details of what facilities are available at regional centres.

Independent care providers

Help at home is available from private and voluntary agencies that offer a range of services, including personal and domestic care, respite facilities, holiday accommodation and companionship. One such organisation, Crossroads Care (see page 206 has schemes in most areas of the country. Charges made by private organisations vary and may be greater than the rates charged by social services. If you wish to obtain care from an independent agency for your relative, or top up the amount of care they receive from the local authority, ask your social worker for details or look in *Yellow Pages*.

Veronica

'As my husband's health got worse we made a family decision about what would be the best thing to do and we all wanted to keep him at home with us. We got help from a private care agency when he needed more care.'

Care homes

Alex

'My father had already been depressed before he went into a home and the staff treated him with good care. We visited several homes before he said that he felt it was the right one for him.'

Care homes offer permanent accommodation to people who are unable to live independently in the community. Many homes also offer respite care facilities and temporary places.

The definition and availability of care changed under the terms of the Care Standards Act (England) 2000 and Regulations of Care (Scotland) 2001; new procedures started everywhere in 2002. All residential and nursing homes are now called 'care homes' with different categories of home available, depending on the types of care offered. Various combinations of care might be offered, for example:

- homes that offer personal care only;
- homes that offer additional nursing care;
- homes that offer personal and nursing care with the facility to provide medicines and medical treatments;
- homes that also cater for people with dementia and those who are terminally ill.

Your relative can purchase all their care needs from private agencies (if they are willing to pay the charge) or, in a few specific instances, if their local authority agrees to give them 'direct payments' to pay directly for the social services that they have been assessed as needing. The principle that nursing care is free in any setting in England since October 2001, and nursing and personal care costs are free in Scotland, since April 2002, still applies.

At the outset of caring you and your relative may be coping well and may not wish to consider these as an option. However, over a period of time, if the care situation becomes stressful or your relative's health deteriorates, moving to a home may become the best or only choice open to you both. In such a situation, it is vital that everyone involved in the decision has a chance to express their feelings about seeking permanent care, provided they are mentally capable. If your relative is able you should discuss with them the merits of staying at home or entering a care home, and weigh up the possible advantages and disadvantages for everyone concerned. Think about all the factors that might influence the decision. For example:

- the benefit of increased safety and care provided by trained staff;
- peace of mind and less stress for the carer, especially if relationships have become strained;
- ready made companionship – but loss of privacy and independence;
- feelings of guilt and the loss of a close relative from the immediate family circle;
- the costs of travel and time;
- the difficulty finding a suitable care home;
- the overall cost of care homes set against charges for care at home;
- could your relative continue to live at home or in 'extra care' housing if the level of services were increased?

Taking the discussion a stage further

It is not easy to decide which type of home to live in and the decision should not be made hurriedly. A list of addresses can be obtained from the local authority, and details can then be obtained direct from individual care homes. Some residential-type homes (whether run by statutory bodies, voluntary organisations or the independent sector) offer living accommodation but do not provide nursing care, so it could be worth considering a home that provides more comprehensive care if you believe that your relative might come to need specialist attention. All types of care homes make charges according to a financial assessment (see page 128), unless your relative has chosen to make their own private contract with the home and pay the full fees. Even if this is the case it is advisable to ask for an assessment from social services to ensure that you are all aware of the options.

Ask around among your friends and acquaintances about the care homes you are considering. Word of mouth is a useful source of information and gives a measure of local feeling about the facilities offered. When you and your relative are getting closer to making a decision, gather together details, draw up a short list and arrange to visit the homes. It is important to 'get a feel' for the atmosphere and care provided. If possible, see if you and your relative can visit to share a meal or other activities with current residents. You might want to ask yourselves some questions to help assess what type of home would be best.

■ How mobile is your relative?
■ What is his/her current physical and mental state and is this likely to change rapidly?
■ How much care and supervision is needed – round the clock cover or day time support only?
■ What type of care is needed – protection and security, nursing care including medication and treatments or personal hygiene care only?
■ Will special aids and equipment be needed?

Remember also the things that your relative likes to do or feels are important, even if they are suffering from depression. For example, if being able to attend a church, enjoy a favourite meal, have regular visitors or walk in the fresh air matter to them (or have done in the past) it is important that they will have the opportunity to continue with these activities.

Registration and inspection

All care homes, whether independent or statutory, are subject to standard registration and inspection procedures, carried out locally. All inspection reports must be publicly available. You can find out more about registration criteria by contacting the local department (contact details will be available at your social services office). Some independent agencies belong to organisations that require them to meet their own independent standards, such as those set by the United Kingdom Home Care Association (UKHCA), in addition to the national criteria set by the Care Standards Act.

Making a complaint

If you are not happy with the services you receive from any organisation (NHS, social services or voluntary agencies) you should try to resolve the situation as soon as possible by speaking to the person involved. This could be the senior person on duty, your care manager or home manager. If you are still not satisfied and wish to take the matter further, contact a customer relations department or equivalent (a voluntary organisation will have a management committee) and ask for details of their complaints procedure. Most NHS Trusts now have a PALS (Patient Advice and Liaison Services) Manager who will be able to help you make a complaint. For independent advice on how to deal with a complaints procedure, contact your local Citizens Advice Bureau. Alternatively, Age Concern runs an Advocacy Service for people over the age of 65 in many areas.

For more *i*nformation

ⓘ Age Concern Factsheet 6 *Finding help at home*

ⓘ Age Concern Factsheet 20 *NHS continuing care, free nursing care and intermediate care.*

ⓘ Age Concern Factsheet 29 *Finding residential and nursing home accommodation.*

ⓘ Age Concern Factsheet 39 *Paying for care in a residential or nursing home if you have a partner.*

ⓘ Age Concern Factsheet 40 *Transfer of assets, and paying for care in a residential or nursing home.*

ⓘ Elderly Accommodation Counsel. Provides a national register of accommodation in the voluntary and private sectors suitable for older people (see page 209).

- 🛈 Independent Healthcare Association. A representative and lobbying organisation for private care homes (see page 210).

- 🛈 Jewish Care. Provides a wide range of social services for the Jewish community, particularly elderly people (see page 211).

- 🛈 United Kingdom Homecare Association. Represents the interests of home care organisations and promotes standards of care. UK helpline provides information on agencies working to the agreed code of practice (see page 217).

- 🛈 For registration and inspection units, look in the local telephone directory, or ask at your social services department or health authority.

Facilities that support home care

Respite care

> **Derek**
>
> 'Having a break was difficult. I went to my daughter for a few days and my wife went into temporary accommodation. We did miss each other but afterwards I felt ready to carry on for a bit longer.'

All carers need a break from caring, to be alone or to spend time with other family members and friends away from the caring situation. This type of break is called 'respite care' and can take many forms, for example:

- a couple of hours out to do some shopping, read a magazine or visit a friend;
- a longer period to take a week-end break or a holiday;
- time spent at home catching up on jobs while your relative goes to a day centre;
- an uninterrupted night's sleep.

Breaks like these are not a luxury. They are essential for your own health and well-being and will help you to cope better. Your relative might also welcome a break from the usual routine. Everyone needs to take time out to 'recharge' their energy levels and reduce the stressload. The Government NHS Plan recognises the importance of respite care in its Better Care – Higher Standards Charter, which indicates that information about 'types of breaks for carers' must be available locally. Even if you feel fine at present, try not to leave it until you are desperate for a break before attempting to make arrangements. Respite care can always be organised if there is an emergency, but it is much better to have a regular time set aside that enables you to plan ahead and have something to look forward to. The effort needed to organise a break may be more than you can take on if you are at crisis point. You might be doubtful about handing your relative over to someone else, even for an hour or so, but the break should be good for both of you. Try to involve your relative in making plans, if at all possible. For example, if there is more than one option, your relative might want to make the choice.

A social worker or community psychiatric nurse would explain about how carers can be assessed for provision of services and can help you make arrangements. Or you can contact the national agencies listed below.

- **British Nursing Association** This agency provides care assistants, home helps and qualified nurses to care for individual people in their own homes. A wide range of services are offered including convalescent care, night care, personal care, shopping, companionship and respite care. The organisation caters for every level of need from occasional visits to live-in care. Look in the telephone directory for a local number or contact the address on page 205.
- **Crossroads Care Schemes** The local schemes are part of a national network set up to provide practical help and support to older people, disabled people and their carers. Each situation is assessed individually with the trained care attendant taking over the role of the family carer. Using the Crossroads Scheme will give you an opportunity for a respite break at a

time of your choosing; care is given 365 days of the year. Look in the telephone directory for a local number or see the address on page 206.

Charges are usually made for respite care. Each organisation will give you details relating to your relative's circumstances. If regular respite care is part of your relative's care from social services, ask them what charges (if any) there might be. People who meet their health authority's criteria for NHS respite health care may have this provided (free of charge) in a hospital or hospice.

Day care

Phyllis

'The ambulance came once a week to take Des to the day centre. He didn't mind going because he realised that I could go out and see a friend or have my hair cut. The social worker set it up for us.'

Day care for your relative is another way for you to have time to yourself, and for your relative to enjoy activities and different company away from their home routine. All local authorities and many voluntary organisations provide day care facilities at specialist (eg for people with dementia) and non-specialist day centres offering a range of social activities and levels of care. Lunch is always provided and, depending on local facilities, your relative might have access to chiropody, hairdressing, complementary therapies, even a bath if this is difficult at home. Or they can sit quietly and rest.

Some services operate in purpose built day centres, while others share accommodation in community centres and residential homes. The staff are trained, professional workers with additional volunteer help in many centres. For more details ask your social worker or community psychiatric nurse.

Continence advice and laundry services

Rhoda

'The district nurse said that my mother was eligible for incontinence pads and the boxes arrived at the door. The pads made such a difference because I had less washing and she slept better because she stopped worrying about wetting the bed.'

If your relative is incontinent, excellent help can be found in most areas through the Continence Advisory Service. Ask at your GP surgery for details. A community nurse or continence adviser will make an assessment. Incontinence has many causes, and it may be possible to improve the symptoms considerably with treatment.

For people who have heavy urine and soiling problems, incontinence pads are available and it may be possible to make use of a home collection laundry service. Facilities vary around the country. Incontinence supplies are free from the NHS, however the quantity of pads supplied may be limited.

For more *i*nformation

ⓘ Age Concern Factsheet 23 *Help with incontinence.*

Meals on wheels

A meals service is provided for older or disabled persons in all areas. It is run by the Women's Royal Voluntary Service, or other local organisation, and these reasonably priced meals are delivered either hot daily or as a pre-packed frozen service at regular intervals. A choice of type is not always available. Referral is via a healthcare professional or the social services.

Extra equipment

Caring for someone at home is likely to become more difficult if the person becomes less mobile. Mobility tends to decline gradually if health and strength fail – unlike the abruptness of paralysis immediately following a stroke for example. So, for you and your relative, each stage can be assessed regularly and you can adjust to whatever degree of movement remains. Aids and equipment to help with moving and handling patients are used frequently by professional carers nowadays as part of Health and Safety regulations. Many useful pieces of equipment can be hired or loaned free of charge from social services, NHS trusts and voluntary organisations.

- **Wheelchair** This is essential for mobility inside and outside the house, especially if your relative has trouble breathing and finds it an effort to walk even short distances.

- **Urine bottle/bedpan** Nowadays many people prefer to purchase these items from a pharmacy or chemist, but bedpans can be borrowed or hired if necessary.

- **Commode** This piece of 'furniture' is necessary in the later stages of an illness but can be useful if your relative needs to use the toilet during the night.

- **Sliding sheets** Made of a slippery nylon fabric, the two surfaces slide easily when placed together to move a person in any direction on chairs, beds and car seats.

- **Moving aids (hand held)** These firm, flat plastic supports can be placed under the thighs or the back of an individual and held by two people to make movement in a bed or chair easier. Alternatively, a banana-shaped board can be placed between a chair and the bed (or wheelchair) to slide the person across so that they do not have to be raised into a standing position. Using aids such as these puts less strain on frail limbs and shoulder joints – for both the patient and their carers.

- **Mechanical hoist** These operate by electric or hydraulic power and are used mainly in care home settings by professional carers for people who are very difficult to move. Hoists can also be recommended for use in the home, after assessment.

- **Bed and chair raisers** These look like heavy-duty, plastic flowerpots and are excellent for raising furniture by several inches to ease the strain of bending and moving.
- **Special mattresses** Several types are available to help protect vulnerable pressure points when a person becomes chair-bound or bed-ridden.
- **Pillow support or back rest** Again, several types are available.
- **Handrails and ramps** These can be positioned at various places, such as the bathroom and at the entrance to the house.
- **Bath aids** Bath aids range from basic non-slip mats to mechanical lifts.
- **Adapted crockery and cutlery** These can be used for general eating and drinking, or for kitchen use if your relative enjoys helping with the cooking or wants to make a hot drink.
- **Two-way 'listening' system, mobile telephone, answering machine or entryphone** All of these offer a means of communication without the need to rush, climb stairs unnecessarily or even be in the same building.
- **Personal alarms** See emergency help systems (page 86).

Derek

'The commode made such a difference. It had wheels so I pushed it right over the toilet seat (without the pot), so there was no need to struggle trying to lift my wife along the landing.'

In all areas of the country, your first point of call for information about equipment loans will be through a community nurse or occupational therapist (OT). An assessment of your relative's need will be arranged. Occupational therapists work towards restoring and maintaining levels of independence and reducing the impact of illness. They may be based with social services or the NHS depending whether your relative has been referred to them because of a health or a social need. Ask the community nurse or your doctor to make a referral for a home visit if you are unsure which agency to approach. Equipment supplied by the NHS is lent free of charge. Unfortunately, waiting lists for certain pieces of equipment are long in many areas.

For more *information*

i The Disabled Living Foundation offers advice on aids and equipment (see page 208).

i Disabled Living Centres Council (see page 208) can tell you the centre nearest you, where you can see and try out aids and equipment.

i The local branches of the British Red Cross or St John Ambulance give advice and arrange the hire or loan equipment. Look in the telephone directory for a contact number or ask the district nurse for a referral.

i Many pharmacist/chemist shops sell aids and small pieces of equipment or keep catalogues for mail order.

i Care and Repair England provides advice and practical help to older and disabled people and those on low incomes, to help them improve their home conditions. Charges are made, but these can be set against a grant if one is provided (see page 205).

Conclusion

The decision whether to look after your relative at home or arrange care in a care home will be based on a number of factors: the wishes of the person concerned; your ability to give quality care; the support that other family members can give; and the type and amount of care that is needed. It is not an easy decision and cannot be taken lightly. Caring for someone else is a time-consuming and strenuous occupation that draws heavily on the personal resources of the main carer. This task is almost impossible to undertake single handed and relies on the support of the professional services as well as family and friends. If the care is long-term, it can put a strain on relationships and stretch finances.

Whatever your initial decision may be, it is important that you review this from time to time and accept that no carer can ever make a promise that is binding forever.

The next chapter will look at helping to manage the financial and legal affairs of an older person.

7 Support with personal affairs

Helping to manage the financial and legal affairs of another person can be one of the main roles of a carer. This can be for one of several reasons: because their relative has become too mentally unwell or physically disabled to manage alone; because they feel unsure about dealing with people in 'authority'; or because they no longer wish to take decisions alone about complex issues. The time span involved in taking over responsibility may be gradual or swift depending on the state of health and wishes of your relative.

This chapter outlines the services and agencies you could turn to for help, and describes some of the welfare benefits and legal procedures that you and your relative may wish to investigate. It is unlikely that you will require all of the information at any one time so return to the relevant sections as necessary during your relative's illness.

Dealing with the affairs of another person is a serious business and you may feel daunted at first. However, there are people who will help you and there are many safeguards in place to protect you and your relative. Always cover yourself by seeking advice from a reputable source – a solicitor, an accountant, a bank or a voluntary organisation – before you enter into legal contracts or make major decisions, especially concerning property or the management of your relative's money, or Power of Attorney/Enduring Power of Attorney.

145

Jeanne

'After my husband was diagnosed with depression I took over our financial affairs. The accountant did our tax self-assessment forms and I talked to the financial adviser about his health insurance policy.'

Finding out about help and advice

Getting the right information needs mental stamina, creative thinking and the investigative skills of Sherlock Holmes – or so it can feel on occasions, particularly if you are tied to the house. With perseverance, however, you can be well informed. Look out for informative articles published by the local and national press and programmes broadcast on radio and television. This type of media material is mostly well researched and aimed at the general public. For more detailed information, advice and advocacy there are many local and national organisations that offer carers a service. Some are specialists in their field while others provide general information and act as signposts to the specialists. Most organisations offer facilities for disabled people and some information is available in minority languages. If time is precious ask a friend to investigate on your behalf. The main agencies to contact are listed in the table opposite.

Charles

'Brenda had always done the day to day household finances so when she wasn't up to it I had to think about budgeting the money. To save myself a journey to the post office I changed our pensions to go straight into the our bank account and set up monthly payments for all the main bills.'

Emily

'When my husband was ill I got in a bit of a muddle paying the bills so my neighbour went with me to the Citizens Advice Bureau and they quickly helped me sort it out.'

Organisation	Services offered	How to contact
Advocacy Services	Independent organisations in most areas that support and develop citizens advocacy work with people who need help controlling their affairs.	Local telephone directory or ask at CAB
Age Concern	Can provide information, support, practical help, social activities and a range of publications for older people and carers.	Local telephone directory or address on page 220
Benefits Agency/ Pensions Service	Provides information on all welfare benefits and processes most local claims.	Local telephone directory
Benefit Enquiry Freephone Line	Provides general advice, information, claim forms and leaflets for disabled people and carers by telephone or post but cannot deal with individual claims.	Tel: 0800 882200 Textphone: 0800 243355
Benefits Advice Centres (Independent)	Independent organisations in many urban areas and some rural areas offering free advice on problems relating to benefits, debt and work issues.	Local telephone directory
Citizens Advice Bureaux	Free, confidential advice and information on a wide range of legal, financial, social and consumer problems and help with form filling and representation at hearings.	Local telephone directory

147

Counsel and Care	Provides free counselling, information and advice for older people and carers including specialist advice about using independent agencies, publishes a range of factsheets and administers trust funds that make payments for equipment and respite care.	Address on page 206
Disability Information Services (called DIAL in some areas)	Advice on aids, and equipment and services	Local telephone directory
Disabled Living Centres Council	Advice on aids and equipment	Address on page 208
Disabled Living Foundation	Advice on aids and equipment	Address on page 208
Help the Aged	Provides a range of services including Seniorline (a free information helpline)	Address on page 209
Housing Advice	Many local councils provide a housing advice service to local residents in private or rented accommodation.	Local telephone directory
Public Library	Excellent sources of local information, books, videos, directories, quality journals and many daily newspapers.	Personal visit, telephone, or limited home delivery

Neighbour-hood Schemes	Many local councils run community schemes offering a range of information and support to local people.	Local telephone directory under Council
NHS Direct	Provides confidential health advice and information, 24 hours a day, seven days a week. Helplines are staffed by qualified nurses and health information advisors.	Telephone 0845 46 47
PALS (Patient Advice and Liaison Service)	Your local Primary Care Trust (the body that is responsible for general practices and family Health services) should have a PALS Manager who you can contact (by telephone initially) for advice.	Ask at your doctor's surgery or health centre

There is also a huge amount of information available on the Internet (see page 62).

State benefits and grants

The benefits system is complex and can only be covered broadly here because each person has individual needs and the information, amounts given and eligibility are subject to change. The Department for Works and Pensions (DWP, formerly the Department of Social Security) is the government agency responsible for social security. The benefits listed below are those most applicable to an older age group. The full range of benefits is listed in leaflets available from the DWP, most local authorities, the Citizens Advice Bureaux and some post offices. Useful ones to look out for are:

■ DWP leaflet SD4 *Caring for someone*, which includes carers' benefits;

■ DWP leaflet FB28SD1 *Sick or disabled?*

For telephone advice about claims and information contact the **Benefits Enquiry Freephone** (see page 147). If you need information about benefits in other languages, contact your local DWP office (listed in the local telephone directory).

People claiming a benefit must meet strict criteria. Some benefits are means-tested, or taxed, or both. If you or your relative disagree with a decision made by the DWP you have the right to appeal and ask for your case to be looked at again. There are strict deadlines for lodging an appeal so, if you are concerned, seek urgent advice.

Benefits Adviser

'Ask about benefits or you won't know what is currently available. It's really worth getting a knowledgeable person to check out your circumstances. Ask for help at the Citizens Advice Bureau.'

Why are people reluctant to claim?

There are millions of pounds of unclaimed benefits, particularly those targeted at older people. Benefits Advisers say that older people and carers are reluctant to claim means tested benefits, and many carers claim on behalf of a relative without realising that they might be eligible for benefits in their own right. The list below gives some reasons why eligible people do not make a claim:

■ they think they are not entitled to money;
■ they don't know what is available;
■ they are too proud and believe that they may be taking money from someone else who is more deserving;
■ they don't want to be bothered with the paperwork;
■ they find the claim forms too complicated.

Benefits Adviser

'Many older people and carers say that they feel too tired and busy to think about benefits. They continue to struggle and try to manage when they may be entitled to make a claim; it's OK to ask for help.'

Benefits for older and/or disabled people

Attendance Allowance

Attendance Allowance is for people aged 65 years or over, whether or not they live alone, who need help with personal care supervision or someone to watch over them. It is tax free and not means tested. But in order to qualify, the person must normally have needed help for a period of six months. If Attendance Allowance is granted, it will be backdated to the date of the claim as long as the six months qualifying period has been satisfied. However, people who are terminally ill qualify immediately. There are two rates according to how much care is needed. Get a claim pack containing Leaflet DS 702 from the DWP office, or by telephoning the Benefits Enquiry Line (see the table on page 147). You could also contact one of the advice agencies (such as the Citizens Advice Bureau), which may be able to help your relative fill it in.

Disability Living Allowance (DLA)

Disability Living Allowance is for people who claim before they reach 65 years of age and who have needed care or had mobility difficulties for more than three months. It has a care component for people who need help with personal care supervision or someone to watch over them, and a mobility component for people who need help with getting around. Disability Living Allowance is tax free and not means tested, nor is it dependent on National Insurance contributions. The person receiving the allowance is free to spend the money however they choose; it does not have to be spent on care. The mobility component has two rates and the care

151

component three; these are awarded according to the needs of the disabled person. People who are terminally ill qualify immediately for the highest rate of the care component. The Disability Living Allowance is a gateway to other types of help, eg the Blue Badge (formerly the Orange Badge) scheme, which gives holders special parking privileges – see Leaflet IB 1.

Incapacity Benefit (IB)

Incapacity Benefit is for people under state pension age who are unable to work because of an illness or disability, and have paid enough National Insurance contributions. The benefit is given at different rates, depending on how long the person has been unable to work. For the first 28 weeks a claimant is assessed on their ability to carry out their own job, based on information given on medical certificates provided by the GP. After 28 weeks the sick or disabled person is assessed on how well they can carry out a range of work related activities, called the Personal Capability Assessment. This assessment is carried out through completion of a questionnaire by the claimant and possibly also an examination by an appointed doctor. Some people may qualify for extra money if their husband or wife is over 60 years or they have dependent children (see Leaflet IB 1).

Benefits for carers

Carers' Allowance (CA)

To qualify for the Carers' Allowance you must be providing care for at least 35 hours per week to a person who is receiving Attendance Allowance *or* Constant Attendance Allowance *or* the middle or highest rates of the care component of Disability Living Allowance. You must be aged 16 or over and under 65 years when you first claim. You cannot get Carers' Allowance if you are in full-time education. You can have a job and still get Carers' Allowance but you must not earn above a certain amount (after deduction of allowable expenses). The allowance is taxable. You may be able to get help with the cost of another carer if you work, and you may be able to get extra money added to other benefits which you are eligible to receive. Carers' Allowance can be backdated for three months (see Leaflet DS 700).

Home Responsibilities Protection

Home Responsibilities Protection is not a benefit but a scheme which helps protect your basic retirement pension. If you are unable to pay National Insurance (NI) contributions or have not paid enough for any year of caring, you can apply for Home Responsibilities Protection, which helps towards qualifying for retirement pension. If you receive Carers' Allowance, you are entitled to National Insurance credits (free contributions on your NI record) and will not usually need Home Responsibilities Protection. If you get Income Support because you are caring for someone, you will usually get Home Responsibilities Protection automatically. If you cannot claim the Carers' Allowance for any reason but still care for over 35 hours per week for someone who receives Attendance Allowance, Constant Attendance Allowance or high or middle rate of the care component of Disability Living Allowance, you may be able to get Home Responsibilities Protection (see Form CF411).

General Benefits

Income Support (Minimum Income Guarantee)

Income Support is a means-tested benefit paid to a person aged 16 years or over whose income is below a certain level and who is not expected to sign on as unemployed. For people over 60 years of age the levels are higher and the benefit used to be described as the 'Minimum Income Guarantee', now replaced by 'Pension Credit' – see overleaf. The person must be incapable of work because of sickness or disability, or bringing up children alone, or aged 60 years and over, or looking after a disabled person or registered blind. Some people who are not in these groups may also qualify for help. Income Support can be paid to top up other benefits or earnings from part-time work (including self-employment), provided the person works fewer than 16 hours per week or if they have no form of income, or they have not paid enough National Insurance contributions. Qualifications for Income Support may be affected by the level of their savings (see Leaflet IS 1).

Pension Credit

Pension Credit is an entitlement for people aged 60 and over, introduced in October 2003. It guarantees that everyone within this age group is entitled to receive a weekly income above a designated level. Two separate levels are available, for single people and people with partners (a partner means a spouse or two people who live together as if married to each other). The person who applies for pension credit must be at least 60 years of age; it does not matter if their partner is under 60.

Pension Credit is also designed to reward people aged 65 and over for a proportion of the savings and income they have for their retirement. In the past older people who had saved towards their retirement were no better off than those who had not saved. Under the terms of Pension Credit a weekly, designated sum of money is available to single people and couples, who qualify.

To qualify for Pension Credit the person is subject to an assessment of weekly net income (after deductions) and savings. Only certain types of income are counted, including: pensions, state benefits (eg Carer's Allowance) and earnings from a job. Types of benefits not subject to means testing are not counted. The amount of savings a person has is taken into account above two separate levels, depending whether the person lives independently or permanently in a care home. Certain groups of people (those who are severely disabled, carers of severely disabled people and those who have certain housing costs) may also be eligible even if their weekly income exceeds the designated amounts (see Leaflet PC1L).

The Social Fund

The Social Fund provides discretionary grants and loans to help people with expenses that are difficult to pay for out of regular income. (Leaflet GL18 covers benefits listed below.)

Budgeting Loans

Budgeting Loans may be available to people receiving Income Support or certain other benefits (for at least 26 weeks) to help spread the cost of important expenses. Interest-free loans (which have to be paid back) may be available for items such as furniture, clothing or to pay travel expenses.

Crisis Loans

Crisis Loans are for people with no savings or access to funds to help them cope with an emergency or disaster, such as fire or a burglary, that puts the family at serious health or safety risk. Applicants do not have to be in receipt of other benefits. The interest-free loan has to be paid back.

Cold Weather Payments

Cold Weather Payments are paid automatically to some recipients of Income Support, including pensioners and disabled people, when the actual or forecast temperature goes down to freezing (zero degrees Celsius) or below for seven consecutive days.

Winter Fuel Payments

Winter Fuel Payment is a one-off annual payment towards the heaviest winter fuel bill. It is normally paid automatically to most people aged 60 years and over, although some need to make an application.

Funeral Payment

Help for funeral expenses is available to some people receiving means-tested benefits, who are responsible for the funeral of a partner, close relative or close friend. The payment may have to be repaid from any money or property left by the person who died. The DWP must agree that it is reasonable for the person to be responsible for the funeral before it will agree any payment, so it is important to check before making arrangements.

Bereavement Benefits

People widowed below pension age may be entitled to bereavement benefits such as the Bereavement Payment or Bereavement Allowance (see Leaflet GL14).

Housing Benefit and Council Tax Benefit

These are worked out in a similar way to Income Support but are administered by the local Council (see below). Savings and some income may affect how much you or your relative can get. Housing Benefit helps tenants pay rent and Council Tax Benefit helps tenants and home owners pay their Council Tax. People receiving Income Support and who claim Housing Benefit or Council Tax Benefit will generally automatically be awarded the maximum amounts (see Leaflet RR2). People receiving other benefits may also qualify.

For more *i*nformation

ℹ Age Concern Factsheet 16 *Income related benefits: income and capital.*

ℹ Age Concern Factsheet 17 *Housing Benefit and Council Tax Benefit.*

ℹ Age Concern Factsheet 18 *A brief guide to money benefits.*

ℹ Age Concern Factsheet 25 *Income Support/Minimum Income Guarantee and the Social Fund.*

ℹ Age Concern Factsheet 34 *Attendance Allowance and Disability Living Allowance.*

ℹ Age Concern Factsheet 48 *Pension Credit.*

ℹ The Pension Service has its own information line: 0800 99 1234 (Textphone: 0800 169 0133). The line is open from 8am – 8pm Monday to Friday and 9am to 1pm Saturday.

NHS benefits

A range of health-related benefits are available for people who receive other state benefits or are on a low income. These might help your relative with charges for prescriptions, eye tests and glasses, dentures and dental treatment, wigs and fabric supports and fares to hospital to receive NHS treatment. Some people (such as those on Income Support) are automatically exempted from some of these charges. Other people on a low income may get help if they apply on form HC1 (except for fares to hospital, which must be claimed from the hospital at each visit). Ask for details at your surgery, hospital clinic or a pharmacy.

For more *information*

i Advisers Guide to help with health costs (NHS booklet HC13).

Taxation

Inland Revenue

Home visits can be arranged for enquiries about personal income and other taxes if your relative is unable to get to a local office. A range of information is available in booklets, many of which appear in other languages, Braille and large print, and in audio cassettes.

Council Tax

Council Tax, collected by local authorities as a contribution towards local services, is assessed according to the value of each property and the number of adults in it. There are reductions, discounts and exemptions available that may help you as a carer and your relative. These relate to empty dwellings (you may have left your home to go and care for your relative or they may have moved in with you), to homes with substantial adaptations that are placed in a lower valuation band, and to people whose presence in a household is disregarded, so leading to a lower bill. Once your Council Tax liability is assessed you or your relative may be able to claim Council Tax Benefit (see above) to help pay. Get help from an advice agency (see the table on page 147) or your local authority.

For more *i*nformation

i Age Concern Factsheet 15 *Income tax and older people.*

i Age Concern Factsheet 21 *Council Tax and older people.*

Grants from private organisations

Many charitable trusts and foundations offer grants to help purchase one-off items of equipment, or pay for respite care. The qualifying criteria vary; for example, a trust fund may be open only to certain categories of people living in a defined area. For information about local and national grant-making organisations try asking at the the Citizens Advice Bureau or public library, or contact Counsel and Care (see page 206) or the National Association of Councils for Voluntary Service (see page 212). Occasionally parish councils administer trusts set up by a local benefactor.

Managing another person's financial affairs

There are several ways that you can take over responsibility for your relative's financial affairs, depending on the state of their physical and mental health status. Their needs may alter rapidly so be ready to increase your level of responsibility and be sure you have set up appropriate procedures before it becomes too late to make changes.

■ **Agents** If your relative is mentally capable, but unable to get out, they can retain overall responsibility for their money but appoint you as their agent. You would be able to cash any pensions and benefits and you may be able to arrange a third party mandate to enable you to deal with bank and building society accounts on their behalf. Ask for details at a post office or bank, as many organisations have a standard application form.

■ **Powers of Attorney** If your relative has financial affairs, you may have to consider a *Power of Attorney*, which is a legal procedure to enable you to deal with their money. The *Ordinary* Power of Attorney can be set up for cases where the person is able to give sound instructions; however, it will become invalid if the person becomes mentally incapable (and can be reviewed if they recover). To avoid this problem, most solicitors suggest an *Enduring* Power of Attorney, which can continue to be used even if your relative becomes too confused to manage their own affairs, provided it is registered with the Public Guardianship Office. It is important that you each take independent advice before setting this up, as it carries a heavy responsibility for the carer that could involve selling property and dealing with taxation. The procedure is very formal so, although not essential, it is usual to act through a solicitor. Further information can be obtained from the Public Guardianship Office (address on page 214).

■ **Court of Protection** If your relative is already 'mentally incapable' the action you can take will depend on their income. For state benefits only, you can become their *appointee*, a procedure that allows you to manage everything to do with their benefits. If the situation is more complex and you do not already have Enduring Power of Attorney you can apply to the Court of Protection. It will appoint a receiver (usually a relative) to manage all the financial business. If you do not wish to undertake this duty, a bank or solicitor will act as receiver in your place. Contact the Customer Services Unit of the Public Guardianship Office (address on page 214).

Managing financial affairs in Scotland

The Adults With Incapacity (Scotland) Act 2000 changed the law relating to the management of financial affairs from April 2001.

159

Individuals can arrange for their welfare to be safeguarded and their affairs to be properly managed in the future, should their capacity deteriorate. They do this by giving another person the Power of Attorney to look after their affairs.

All continuing and welfare Powers of Attorney granted after April 2001 will need to be registered with the Public Guardian Office to be effective. Individuals can also apply to the Public Guardian Office to access the funds of an adult incapable of managing these funds. From April 2002, authorised care establishments can manage a limited amount of funds and property of residents who are unable to do this for themselves.

For more *i*nformation

i See the Scottish version of Age Concern Factsheet 22 _Legal arrangements for managing financial affairs._

Making a will

Depression Alliance

'Death is always a difficult subject to deal with but making a will and other financial arrangements can save a lot of heartache in the long run.'

When someone is ill, they begin to think more about their personal affairs and may ask you to help them sort out the legal arrangements. Your relative may talk to you about making a will, or they may wish to add to or alter an existing will, if their situation has changed. If you feel uncomfortable or unsure about doing this task, ask someone else to help — perhaps a friend who is sensible and practical but less personally involved. If your relative is unable to go out, many solicitors offer a home service to help people write a will. Look in the *Yellow Pages* or ask at the Citizens Advice Bureau for details.

Some people draw up their own wills. This is quite in order as long as the correct procedures are followed. The will must be written clearly, and signed and dated in the presence of two (or just one in Scotland) independent witnesses or relatives who are not beneficiaries, and must not be married to a beneficiary. The will must name at least one person who is willing to act as an executor – the people responsible for seeing that the instructions written in the will are properly carried out. Executors can be relatives, friends or professional people, who provide this service as part of their job (eg an accountant or a solicitor). A person who acts as an executor can also be named in the will as a beneficiary. Information packs and will forms are available from most stationers, and details of other booklets are given below. (If you live in Scotland make sure that the information covers the law in Scotland.) If your relative's affairs are not simple or straightforward, it would be wise to ask a solicitor to draw up the will. Solicitors' fees for home and office appointments vary, so telephone and ask for a price guide before booking a home visit.

Why is making a will important?

Some people wrongly assume that if their affairs are straightforward they do not need to make a will, because all of their belongings will go directly to their closest relative. But there are strict laws about how a person's estate (the name given to their possessions) is divided up and it can be complicated and costly to sort out the affairs of someone who has not made a will (is intestate).

The following sensible comments from a solicitor should help if your relative is undecided and asks your opinion about the benefits of making a will.

> ■ 'You don't have to have a lot of money to make a will. Making a will is about making sure that your possessions go to the person(s) you want to receive them.'
>
> ■ 'You mustn't feel morbid about making a will; all you are doing is setting out your plan as to how your assets are to be split up when you die.'
>
> ■ 'If you do not make a will the rules governing intestacy apply, which may mean that your assets will be given to relatives you do not know or even want to know.'
>
> ■ 'Just saying to someone that a treasured ornament or a piece of jewellery is theirs when you die is not good enough. The only safe way of making sure that happens is to put it in a will.'

Registering a death

A death should be registered in the district where the death occurred, within five days, unless the Registrar says this period can be extended. The person registering the death can make a formal declaration giving the details required in any registration district in England and Wales. This will then be passed to the Registrar for the district where the death occurred, who will issue the death certificate and any other documentation. (In Scotland, the death can be registered in the office for the area where the deceased person normally lived). Some offices operate an appointment system, so telephone as soon as you receive the Medical Certificate of Cause of Death. Whether the death occurs in a hospice or at home you will be given the same type of Certificate. The address and telephone number of the local office are in the telephone directory; leaflets are available from the office.

In certain circumstances the death will be referred to the Coroner. If this is the case you will be advised what to do. A Coroner is usually involved when the death is sudden, unnatural, unexplained or attended by suspicious circumstances. A common reason is because the GP has not seen the deceased within the last 14 days.

Two free certificates are given to enable the funeral arrangements to be made, but as many organisations (eg banks and insurance companies) require a certificate to complete their business it would be wise to buy extra copies.

It is usual for the death to be registered by a relative but it can be another person. Allow a reasonable amount of time to complete the formalities and it helps to have certain pieces of information to hand. The Registrar will want to know the following information about the deceased person:

- the date and place of death;
- their full name (and maiden name if appropriate);
- their date and place of birth;
- their occupation and that of the husband for a married women or widow;
- their usual address;
- whether they were in receipt of a pension from public funds;
- the date of birth of their spouse if appropriate;
- their NHS number or actual medical card if available.

Certificates

There are three types of certificates issued by the Registrar depending on who must be told of the death. By law, Registrars cannot issue the necessary certificates unless they are certain beyond all reasonable doubt that the death is above suspicion, particularly if the body is to be cremated.

- **A Certificate for Burial or Cremation (Green Form)** This is supplied for the funeral director who cannot proceed without it. The certificate is free of charge.
- **A Certificate of Registration of Death** This is supplied for social security purposes. Relatives are asked to read the details on the reverse of the form and return it to the local DWP office if any circumstances applies to the deceased person, for example if they were in receipt of a state pension or welfare benefits. This certificate is free of charge.
- **Standard Death Certificates**. These are issued for use by banks, building societies, insurance companies and any such

163

organisation that requires official notification. It may be wise to buy additional copies at the time of registration as they cost more if a relative re-applies.

For more *i*nformation

ⓘ Age Concern Factsheet 7 *Making your Will.*

ⓘ Age Concern Factsheet 14 *Probate: dealing with someone's estate.*

ⓘ Age Concern Factsheet 27 *Arranging a funeral.*

ⓘ Age Concern Factsheet 22 *Legal arrangements for managing financial affairs.*

ⓘ Benefits Agency booklet D49, *What to do after a death* is available from Department for Work and Pensions offices or local probate registry offices.

ⓘ The Consumers' Association offer a range of useful information booklets and packs about all aspects of making and dealing with wills (see page 206 for address).

ⓘ Contact the local probate registry office (see telephone directory) for information about how to obtain probate. Leaflets are available.

Conclusion

This chapter has covered a wide range of services, available from many organisations and agencies in the private, public and voluntary sectors. If you have read through the chapter briefly, you may then find it useful to return to the appropriate section when the time is right, as your circumstances change.

8 Stress relief for carers

Caring for someone who is unwell is stressful for many reasons. The over-riding sadness of dealing with a mental health illness, anxieties about the future and the extra pressures of trying to manage your own life alongside caring for your relative all contribute towards emotional and physical fatigue. It is no wonder most carers say that feelings of tension rarely go away.

This chapter describes the main elements of stress and helps you focus on your personal problems. How you deal with a difficult situation depends on all sorts of factors – your personality type, how much control you feel, and how much energy you have in reserve – can all play their part in your ability to cope.

Everyone needs a few strategies to draw upon when it is important to be mentally strong or reduce tension. This chapter looks at ways to build up your personal strengths and develop some support systems. It offers a selection of coping skills to use when you feel at the end of your tether yet need to remain calm. Relaxing your muscles or enjoying an aromatherapy massage can work wonders when you are feeling pressured and over tired.

The advice given in the chapter is intended to help you make use of self-help techniques that will help you deal with everyday problems, some of which might stem from your caring role. It must be acknowledged, however, that if your relative's illness is at the root of your distress, stress reducing strategies may help with daily living but they cannot take away that hurt.

What is 'stress'?

Janet

'I have never felt so uptight in my life before. I feel like an over-stretched elastic band – ready to snap.'

The word 'stress' is very popular nowadays, and is commonly used to describe the way we feel when pressure is intense. It is not a medical problem but a combination of symptoms produced when our physical, mental and emotional systems go into overdrive. Everyone's body reacts to stress in the same physical way, whatever the cause or size of the problem. Unfortunately, though, some people seem to get more upset than others when faced by difficult situations. This stronger reaction to stress is often produced by a combination of factors – the person's emotional state at the time, their inherent personality type and how well they have learned to cope in the past – rather than the extent of the problem.

High stress levels for carers are likely to stem from:

- loneliness and isolation;
- shortage of time;
- uncertainty about the future;
- difficult relationships and pressures from other people;
- feeling that life is getting out of control;
- lack of sleep;
- feeling under valued and over worked;
- lack of knowledge.

Primitive feelings

Kate

'I developed such dreadful migraines and they always followed stressful episodes.'

Coping with day-to-day stress is normal because a small amount of pressure can improve performance. It keeps your brain stimulated and helps you concentrate and deal with challenging situations. For example, many actors regard a bit of stress as essential: it adds sparkle to their performance and keeps them alert. But when the pressure becomes too great, the physical reaction can be unpleasant. As tension builds up, your body produces high levels of the hormone adrenaline to prepare itself for action in the same way as a primitive caveman. This reaction, known as the 'fight or flight' mechanism, enabled him to respond swiftly to danger. For us, however, unlike our ancestors, this type of 'escape' is rarely necessary. So instead of using up the energy generated to deal with the hazard (stressful situation) it remains in the system, keeping it in a continual state of tension. While adrenaline levels are high, you probably feel as if you are living on the edge of a crisis so it takes little additional worry to make you feel very anxious. The tension can become so intense that you may feel as if you are about to explode and you can no longer handle all of the demands being made of you. If you 'listen' to your body it is telling you that it feels extremely distressed.

Paul

'My partner was very depressed and I had to keep working as well as spending time with him. I am the manager in a large company and it was coming up to the festive time of the year. The thought of being jolly filled me with dread.'

> ### Wendy
> 'When my father was ill I had my mother-in-law to support as well. My husband works away from home and I would have given anything for an offer of help from someone.'

Warning signs

> ### Janet
> 'When my father had not taken his tablets yet again I nearly exploded. Why couldn't he remember when I had put them right on the kitchen table? I'd had a huge delay in a traffic jam, my head was aching and I wanted a bit of peace.'

> ### Kate
> 'When my boss started checking on my time off I felt frustrated and angry with her; she knew my mother was ill, why couldn't she be more flexible?'

The signs and symptoms that indicate that you might be feeling over stressed are triggered by a combination of physical and emotional reactions. Look at the list below and note the ones that trouble you regularly. If you are bothered by more than a few the time is right to consider some solutions before your own health begins to suffer:

- headaches;
- listlessness and fatigue;
- difficulty in sleeping at either end of the night;
- palpitations and rapid pulse rate;
- indigestion or heartburn;
- breathing problems (particularly if breathing becomes faster and shallower);
- aching joints;

- eating too much or not enough;
- skin problems;
- increased need to pass urine, and nervous diarrhoea;
- numbness or pins and needles in limbs;
- poor concentration and difficulty making decisions;
- feeling unhappy and depressed;
- feeling angry, frustrated and helpless;
- feeling irritable and tearful;
- anxiety and fearfulness;
- loss of sense of humour.

Where do all the stresses come from?

Richard

'My wife tried to protect me even though she was ill but knowing that made me feel worse. I felt that I had to be strong for both of us.'

Suzanne

'I nearly collapsed the day the car wouldn't start. Tension was building up with no time to think. I called the garage and cried with exhaustion – I felt ashamed at my lack of control.'

It is difficult to define stress clearly because it feels as if it comes from two directions, both external and internal. The confusion arises when we talk about stress as a *cause* of problems (pressures from people or situations) and as an *effect* (a response from inside our bodies, such as a tension headache). Both internal and external stresses affect our moods and the physical ability to cope. Unfortunately, not all sources of stress are within our control, and problems can rarely be packaged neatly into distinct 'causes'. Mostly we manage to keep the troubles isolated and give our bodies sufficient rest before dealing with next set of problems, but when you are caring for another person this may not always be possible.

Psychologists refer to these sources of stress as 'life events' and they include major upheavals like retirement, moving home, changing job, an accident and illness, but also lesser events such as Christmas or going on holiday. They aren't particularly special or rare and they aren't necessarily unpleasant, just things that happen to all of us all of the time. However, if a string of events happen too close together, pressure builds up to uncomfortable levels and it only takes one small problem to bring everything to a head. The important point to note is that it is the *accumulation* of both major and minor events coming together that creates the worse scenario, rather than merely the severity of the events.

Stress triggers

Paul

'It was hot and humid, the fan went wrong and I had to collect the prescriptions before the pharmacy closed. I tried to ignore the panicky feeling caused by too little time and no lunch.'

If the build up of tension has already reached a critical level, it won't take much to tip you over the top. Do the following 'nerve janglers' seem familiar?

- Tiredness caused by insufficient sleep due to frequent interruptions in the night, or altered sleep patterns such as waking early.
- Prolonged pain perhaps from aching joints or the continual physical strain of helping an older person move around.
- Fragile emotions stemming from anger, sadness or anxiety.
- Frustration and pressures created by people or places – demanding relatives, hospital appointments, shopping in crowded supermarkets.
- Discomfort caused by lack of fresh air, too much noise or feeling too hot or too cold.
- Depressing weather – some people are adversely affected by too little sunlight and long dark evenings.

- Sensitive digestive system – too much alcohol, caffeine in tea and coffee or refined sugar can all exacerbate stress.
- Craving for a cigarette because anxiety levels are high. Stress is the reason many people give for continuing to smoke.
- Uncertainty about the future and possible financial worries.
- Impatient personality – some people tend to be quicker to react than others.

Two personal stories

Ailsa and Maureen share their stories, both of which demonstrate how stress builds up into distress.

Ailsa

'My husband and I had just set up our own business when my father was diagnosed with depression. The next few months were a nightmare. I felt that my time and my loyalties were divided, causing a great deal of anxiety. I went to the surgery with him while he saw the doctor, visited him while he was in hospital for a couple of weeks and then rushed back to do the paperwork for our business. I still felt worried after he settled back at home because I didn't know how well he was caring for himself. I couldn't sleep because I was uncertain about the future and began to feel unwell with quite a lot of physical and emotional symptoms – bad headaches, extreme tiredness, poor appetite and feelings of panic. The final straw came when our house was burgled. I felt completely shattered and didn't know where to turn for help.'

Maureen

'I had been taking care of my mother for several months after my father had died because she was feeling low and I was beginning to feel that I couldn't carry on. Besides looking after her, the rest of my life threw up the usual problems. I had to teach my class at the secondary school, mark pupils' work in the evenings and support my daughter who was taking her final exams at college. I was very tempted to start smoking again

171

even though I had given up several years earlier. The situation came to a head one day when I exploded at my class, treating a minor event like a major disaster. When the situation had calmed down I was left feeling drained, trembling and confused at the strength of my own emotions. Fortunately, a colleague at school persuaded me that I needed help. I went to my GP, who arranged for me to see a qualified counsellor within the practice. It helped enormously to talk to someone who listened without passing judgement.'

Ailsa and Maureen had each gone through a difficult period in a short space of time with a run of problems adding to their stress load. Each story illustrates a pattern that can lead to a build up of pressure:

- a series of stressful events close together;
- little control over the individual situations;
- burden from other people;
- little time for personal relaxation.

Maureen was lucky to have had a caring colleague who recognised the signs of stress and suggested she seek help. She found a safety valve by talking to a counsellor. Be aware of early warning signs and learn how to recognise your own body's signals so that you can help yourself before you reach discomfort level. Unfortunately, there is no magic formula. Stress management – like any other skill – needs to be learned and practised.

Getting the balance right

The key to managing stress is getting the balancing act right between tension and relaxation – like a juggler if you get too many plates in the air at once they all come crashing down. Caring brings extra responsibilities. If you are the main person your relative relies on, balancing your own needs against theirs may be hard to achieve. Unfortunately, you are the one most likely to end up with too much stress and too little time for relaxation. Tension and anxiety can't be switched off to order but this does not mean they should be ignored as being over-stressed could cause you to become depressed yourself. There are ways to ease the pressure and give your body a rest, and stress is easier to bear if you understand and accept where the problems are coming from.

Maureen

'I have learned that I am not superhuman so I think about what jobs need tackling and I divide them into those that are urgent and those that can wait. It is amazing how my mind clears when I have sorted out the priorities.'

Paul

'When I stop and reflect on how I coped – I know that I tried to keep each part of my life separate. While I was supporting my partner I put work to the back of my mind and while I was at work I did what I had to do and delegated some of the load to others.'

Stress diary

Writing a stress diary can help to sort out where some of the pressures are coming from. It may seem like yet another task but a few minutes spent now may save you from sleepless hours later. Start the process by making a list of all the things that have bothered you in the last week. Next jot down by the side of each problem how you felt at the time – angry, anxious, irritable etc. Now circle the things that you chose to do willingly – they may have been difficult, but if you accept their importance you are less likely to be upset by the effort. Look at the remainder of the problems on your list and ask yourself if they could be the cause of your increased anxiety. Are they stemming from external pressure over which you have little control? The reason why many people get angry and upset about some situations and not others is often linked to their feelings about choice. Can you cross out anything off your list to ease the pressure?

Phyllis

'My husband Des needs care. I want to look after him at home for as long as I am able, however difficult. We are very close and I believe it helps his depression if he is in familiar surroundings with the grandchildren nearby and his beloved garden outside.'

Because Phyllis has made a personal decision to care for her husband, she feels calmer about the outcome.

Richard

'I wanted to be at home to take care of my wife when she became more depressed so the decision to take early retirement was mine, but I did miss the company and social life of the office. While my wife goes to her sister one day a week I always spend that time following my own hobbies. I play bowls or go to the snooker club – whatever I fancy.'

Mental stimulation

Stress doesn't always arise from over-activity. It is also possible to feel frustrated and unsettled if you are bored, isolated at home and doing the same repetitive jobs day after day – a scenario which might sound familiar to carers. It is unrealistic to believe you can exercise control over every aspect of your life, but at least try to manage your respite time to counteract the daily turmoil. For example, if there is pressure at home choose a relaxing pastime. Don't take on extra responsibilities outside of the house or engage in strenuous activities. If you are isolated at home arrange to spend respite time in pleasant company, perhaps involving some interesting conversation.

Helping yourself

By now you've probably got a clearer picture about the main causes of your stress and feel ready to make some changes that will help you to cope. Start the process by asking yourself how you dealt with difficult situations in the past and what lessons you learned from that process. Then think about what is different this time round and what steps might be needed to help you get along. Remember that problems are rarely solved in isolation so think about who (or what) you could turn to for support. Finally, accept that not all problems can be 'solved'. Your relative's illness may not disappear entirely, but you can do your best to deal with it in the best way possible.

Finding ways to cope with pressure

No one ever 'cured' their stress overnight – so don't rush into hasty decisions. Look at each problem separately with four courses of action in mind:

- **One** Is it necessary to change the situation? This course may call for major action, such as moving your relative into a care home. Making a decision of this nature will be extremely upsetting so do not attempt to make it alone. But if you are finding it very difficult to cope, it could be the right longer term solution.
- **Two** Can you improve your ability to deal with the situation? Your stress levels might fall quite dramatically if you ease some of the pressure on yourself and your time. A practical solution, such as getting help with the housework, could be the answer.
- **Three** Do you need to change your perception of the situation? Ask yourself if the problem is as bad as you think it is (the immediate problem that's worrying you right now or the longer term effects of the depression) and try to turn some of the threats into challenges. Positive 'self-talk' works well here, tell yourself that you have dealt with difficult situations before and that you have ample reserves of inner strength.

175

■ **Four** Would changing your routine help? Doing things through habit is easy, especially if you are feeling upset, but your routine may be increasing your stress. If you are rushing around frantically, slow down so that your actions become calmer. This gives your brain a less-stressed message. Cut down on the amount of coffee and tea you drink; the caffeine they contain stimulates the nervous system causing irritability and insomnia. Change any routines which are particularly tiring; for example, avoid shopping at the supermarket at busy times.

Emily

'I spend a small amount of money getting the lawn cut to ease the burden. My husband used to do all the practical jobs, but I was grateful when my neighbour did some decorating and we use hospital transport to get to the clinic.'

Derek

'My daughter lives nearby and she sits down with me each evening and we talk over what jobs need doing the next day. I can sleep better if I have sorted out in my mind what to do before the care assistant arrives to help my wife get up.'

Personal resources

Maureen

'My mother isn't going to get any younger and I have to continue working. So after my outburst I felt concerned about my state of mind. I must have a bit of space for myself or I wouldn't be able to carry on. I went to see a counsellor and she helped me draw up a list of my main strengths and encouraged me to draw on the support of people I trust. It was very reassuring to think about all of my personal resources.'

Maureen's list included things that she really values:

- a firm relationships with husband, children, family and friends;
- good physical health;
- a positive mental attitude (Maureen usually feels confident and enjoys her job);
- a sense of humour;
- financial security;
- spiritual support;
- non-dependence on smoking, alcohol or drugs.

Maureen's counsellor encouraged her to think about where she could help herself further. You might find this a useful exercise to do yourself.

Maureen

'Together my counsellor and I agreed I could improve my ability to cope by:

- finding more time for myself and having a relaxing hobby;
- learning to say 'no' sometimes;
- cutting back on some of the household jobs that are not a high priority.'

Like Maureen, you could start by identifying your strengths and thinking about where you feel vulnerable. Then talk to someone you trust about the steps you could take to improve the areas where you feel insecure, at least to the point where you feel less anxious. Take each step gently, this is not a time to push yourself.

Ailsa

'I've learned not to keep it all bottled up, and meet with friends regularly. We rarely talk about my worries, but I know I can when I need to, and it helps occasionally.'

Maureen

'It never crossed my mind that I could ask for counselling. I had always thought that counselling was for people who couldn't deal with life. How wrong I was – four sessions with a trained counsellor made all the difference to how I coped.'

Finding support

Any support is valuable when you are feeling under pressure, especially if it is undemanding. Asking for help is not a sign of weakness; it is more a demonstration of awareness that problems can seldom be solved alone. If you are beginning to feel depressed yourself it is vital you seek help. You may need to make the first move with friends and relatives by asking for a listening ear, as they may be reticent to 'interfere' unless invited. Once you have given the signal to initiate help, you should discuss with the other person how this can be achieved without upsetting your relationship. It is important to agree a few basic rules at the beginning, because the last thing you want is someone marching in and taking over. For example, the person you talk to must respect your need for confidentiality. They need to be aware that you may become emotional and let off a 'bit of steam'. Also, you must feel free to ignore their advice without fear of causing offence.

If talking to a friend or relative is not the best course for you (because you would find this uncomfortable or there isn't a suitable person) other options are available. Ask your doctor or the community psychiatric nurse about:

- specialist services which offer stress counselling, psychological and/or spiritual support;
- self-help and carers' groups run by social services, health trusts, mental health charities or at a carers' centre;
- private counsellors (be sure they are trained and registered);
- religious leaders;
- telephone helplines (eg most mental health charities, or CarersLine 0808 808 7777 run by Carers UK);

■ Samaritans (the national 24-hour helpline staffed by trained counsellors who offer emotional support to people who are feeling isolated and in despair – 08457 909090 or see local telephone directory).

Learning to relax

Phyllis

'The doctor suggested a group at the carers' centre. I was unsure at first, but I found that although it didn't change the fact that my husband is ill, I coped better with it all. We always ended with a relaxation session and I went home feeling calm and supported. A volunteer from a charity sat with my husband.'

Decreasing the tension

If your body is already feeling tired and strained any movements that increase muscular tension are an extra drain on your energy reserves so it is worth being as relaxed as possible. Ask a friend to observe your general posture or catch sight of yourself in the mirror or a shop window. Look out for uncomfortable positions and bad habits, such as:

■ head thrusting forward or bent down with your chin hard on your chest;
■ shoulders hunched and rounded;
■ arms held tightly across your chest or stiffly by your sides with hands clenched;
■ legs crossed over and twined together;
■ restless habits such as tapping fingers and feet, or hair twisting;
■ nail biting and teeth clenching.

Better breathing

Breathing is an unconscious action that you rarely think about, but over the years you may have developed poor breathing habits

179

without realising their significance. Irregular breathing patterns (such as hyperventilation or overbreathing) can increase anxiety levels. When your body is calm, breathing is slow, regular and deep, but when anxiety levels are high the opposite happens, breathing becomes fast, irregular and shallow, creating feelings of panic. Breathing is normally controlled by the involuntary nervous system but it is possible to take control of the process and calm the system down when pressure begins to rise. People who learn to breathe calmly when they are feeling tense soon notice an improvement in their anxiety state. The following guidelines will help remedy overbreathing and generally reduce tension:

- As soon as anxiety levels begin to rise, quietly tell yourself to 'calm down'. This sends a positive message to the brain.
- Slow down all your movements, because rushing around increases agitation and your body responds by producing more adrenaline to deal with the 'threat'.
- Calm your breathing deliberately and keep an even rhythm with a slight pause between the in and out breaths; imagine a candle in front of your face which gently flickers as you breathe out.
- Practice calm breathing at different times during the day so that you are aware of the feeling of taking control. It is much easier to recognise the correct pattern when you are not over anxious.

Ailsa

'I found that once I had learned to control my breathing I became more relaxed generally. The uptight feeling went away and I felt less agitated.'

Deep relaxation

Deep relaxation is an excellent way to restore energy and boost your spirit but it does need time and space. Merely telling yourself to relax is unlikely to work, especially if you are feeling over-wrought. Relaxation is easy to learn but it does requires practice; it may take several sessions to get it right and it helps if you understand how the technique works. It is all about fooling the system and giving out positive signals that your body is at ease. Relaxed muscles and slow, quiet breathing send calming messages to the brain that turns off the false reaction to danger. When there are no threats, your body rests and restores itself ready for the next burst of energy.

Whole body relaxation

This is the most common form of relaxation and produces pleasant results quickly. The technique always works if you create the right conditions and allow sufficient time – about 20 minutes for a whole body session. Eventually, you can cut down on the time and recreate the stress-free feeling anywhere as you improve your skill. If you would like to learn to relax with a teacher, ask at your GP surgery or health centre. Many stress counsellors run individual or group classes.

Step by step technique for use at home

1 Find a warm, quiet place and lie on a rug or sit in a well supported chair. Use a pillow for support if it helps to make you more comfortable. Reduce outside noises if possible.

2 Wear loose clothing and remove glasses and shoes. Lie on your back with your head supported, and your arms and legs straight and slightly apart.

3 Breathe in and out deeply for three breaths and imagine you are loosening the tension; then breathe normally.

4 You can close your eyes at this stage or wait until they shut naturally. You are going to work on each major muscle group starting with the feet. As you tighten and relax the muscles learn to recognise the difference between tension and relaxation. Hold each constriction for a few seconds and repeat each action with a short break between.

5 Pull your feet towards your body – hold the tension – release and feel the reduction in tension.

6 Point your toes hard away from your body and feel the tension in your calf muscles – hold – and relax

181

7 Next work on your thighs by drawing your legs tightly towards you or raising them into the air – hold – drop back to a relaxed position with thighs rolled outwards.

8 Tense your buttocks by squeezing them hard together – hold – and relax.

9 Tense your abdomen in the opposite way by pushing it outwards – hold – and then let it flop.

10 Check your legs again and if you have slipped back into a tense position have a second go from step 5. A couple of deep breaths will help at this point. Your lower body should feel heavy, warm and relaxed.

11 Now concentrate on your back. Arch your spine away from the floor or chair – hold – and relax. (**Warning:** leave this one out if you have any back problems.)

12 Now move your shoulders backwards to expand your chest – hold – and relax.

13 Tense your shoulders next by raising your arms and pulling on your shoulders – hold – as you drop your arms wriggle your shoulders up to your ears and relax with your shoulder blades touching the floor or chair.

14 Now work on your hands and lower arms by making a tight fist – hold – and relax letting your fingers droop. As you clench your fists for the second time raise your arms slightly off the ground and notice the tension in your forearms – hold – and relax.

15 Move to the upper arms by bringing your hands across your body, close to your chest – hold – relax them to a position on the floor with the palms facing upwards.

16 Relax your neck and throat by gently moving your head from side to side (not a circular movement) and then pulling your chin down to your chest – hold – and relax.

17 Next clench your jaw by clamping your teeth together – hold – and let go so that your mouth is slightly open. That tension probably felt familiar as clenching teeth is a common habit.

18 Now work on your facial muscles. Press your lips together – hold – and relax. Push your tongue hard to the roof of your mouth – hold – and let it drop to the floor of your mouth.

19 Move your eyes inside your closed lids to the four quarters of a circle and then let your eyelids relax.

20 Finally relax your forehead and scalp. Frown hard and pull your forehead down – hold – and let go so that your face feels loose.

Your whole body should now feel comfortable and free from tension. Breathe gently and let your mind wander at will. If stressful thoughts irritate you in this relaxed state, think about somewhere pleasant and, as you breathe, repeat in you mind 'peace in and pressure out'. Don't worry if you drop off to sleep at this point. Eventually you will learn to relax your body without going to sleep, but use this method at night if insomnia is a problem.

Lie quietly with your eyes closed for a few minutes enjoying the warm feeling; then slowly bring yourself back to the present. Count backwards from five to one, clench your fists tightly, relax and rub your hands together. If you are lying on the floor roll onto your side; open your eyes with you hands shielding them from the light. Stand up slowly and try to hold on to the relaxed mood when you return to action.

Getting the best from relaxation

Sharing the session with another person is pleasant. You can take turns to read the instructions or make yourselves a tape recording. Listen to music if it helps to calm your mind and ring the changes by starting at the top and working towards your feet. As you become better at 'switching off', shorten the session and create a relaxed mood by imagining your body is warm and heavy without going through all of the muscle tightening steps. Use this shortened version as a mini-restorative, particularly when you are away from home in stressful situations.

For more *i*nformation

ⓘ Addresses in the 'Useful addresses' section at the end of the book.

ⓘ British Association for Counselling publishes a directory of counsellors in UK.

ⓘ Family Doctor Series of booklets: *Understanding Stress*, available from most chemist shops.

ⓘ Music tapes: *The Fairy Ring* and *Silver Wings*, both by Mike Rowland, and *Spirit of the Rainforest* by Terry Oldfield are soothing tapes to use for relaxation. They are available from music shops or by catalogue from New World Aurora.

ⓘ The Stress Management Training Institute publishes a wide range of materials to help reduce stress: leaflets, audio tapes, books and a newsletter.

ⓘ The Royal College of Psychiatrists publishes a range of information for dealing with anxieties, phobias, depression and bereavement. Send a stamped addressed envelope with your request.

Complementary treatments to help with stress

Veronica

'While my husband was at his day centre my sister treated me to a weekly aromatherapy session – it was wonderful. I would never have done such a thing on my own but we went along together.'

The terms 'alternative therapy' and 'complementary therapy' are used to describe a range of treatments available from practitioners and therapists who work to treat the whole body, either alongside, or instead of, treatments offered by conventional medicine. In order to clarify the difference in meaning, the following descriptions are commonly accepted.

■ **Conventional medicine** This covers a range of treatments which your relative may have already received, including medication and orthodox therapies (such as ECT) which have been widely used throughout the world for many years and have undergone expert clinical trials.

- **Unconventional medicine** This covers a number of treatments that are widely used and, on the whole, widely respected. Included in this group are homeopathy and herbal medicine. Practitioners do not claim the medications used will cure depression but the treatments may help to reduce the symptoms caused by the disorder and the side effects of orthodox treatments.
- **Complementary therapies** These are therapies intended for use *alongside* (as a 'complement' to), orthodox medicine rather than replacing it. Examples include physical treatments such as aromatherapy and reflexology, and 'talking' therapies, such as counselling and psychotherapy, that benefit the person's state of mind. The treatments may be beneficial both for you and for your relative as complementary therapies can help to combat tension and stress and give a welcome boost to your morale.
- **Alternative therapies** These therapies are usually held to be treatments that are given *instead* of conventional treatments. These therapies often involve regimens that attempt to treat the illness direct, using non-medical methods. Most alternative treatments have not been subjected to clinical trials.

Many popular complementary treatments originated in the East and have been practised there for centuries. They rely on ancient knowledge linked to herbal remedies and traditional practices that are believed to stimulate the body's own healing powers. Acupuncture from China and yoga from India are obvious examples. Some of the newer therapies appeal more to Western scientific minds and are used as aids to diagnosis as well as treatment. Two examples are colour therapy, that draws links between certain colours and mental harmony or stress, and iridology that examines the eyes for clues to hidden disorders.

All complementary and alternative treatments can be obtained without going to a medically trained doctor, but this does not mean that an NHS or private doctor will not or cannot provide some complementary treatments. Some doctors are dually trained and many GPs now recommend the benefits of such therapies. Increasingly, complementary therapies are being introduced into the NHS and are available at day centres and GP practices, either free of charge or with a fee. Geographical location may affect your ability to find a suitable practitioner; ask at your local library, GP surgery or health centre.

A note of caution: before using any complementary or alternative therapy with your relative, especially if they are receiving other medication and treatments, it is extremely important to consult with their doctor. There are several reasons for seeking advice before starting a non-orthodox treatment:

■ some therapies use extracts from plants that can have very powerful properties which may affect other treatments;
■ the effort of being massaged may be too tiring for a frail body;
■ and some therapies use methods that have not been scientifically tested.

There is some conflict of opinion between supporters of conventional medicine and supporters of alternative therapies. Many doctors providing orthodox treatment are concerned that alternative cures may be harmful. Patients sometimes reject conventional medicine and seek alternative remedies out of a false sense of hope and promises of amazing cures. There is no justifiable evidence that such cures exist and no reputable therapist would ever make such claims.

Finding a qualified therapist

Several of the therapies described in this chapter can be practised at home using basic remedies and techniques learned from a book. If you use information from a book to prepare treatment materials be sure to follow the instructions carefully. However, rather than spend time learning new techniques you and your relative may prefer to receive treatment from a qualified practitioner. Some alternative therapies cannot be recommended for self-help practice and it is advisable that treatment is obtained only from a trained practitioner. Ask for details of reputable, local therapists at your GP surgery or health centre. Alternatively, you could contact the national organisations listed in the sections 'For more information'. Word of mouth can be a good form of recommendation but do make sure any therapist you visit is registered to practice with the appropriate national body.

Don't be embarrassed to ask directly about qualifications, as all trained therapists will be pleased to offer reassurance and tell you how to check. Properly trained therapists take a full medical history before prescribing. They will have learned about the effects of the remedies they use, whereas untrained people can only guess and may do harm. There are some ready made treatments available in health shops, but it would be wise to consult a doctor first, before taking any over-the-counter medication, so you do not delay diagnosis or effective orthodox treatment. Finally, whichever complementary or alternative treatment you choose, it is wise to consult a medical doctor if symptoms persist.

You and your relative may be sceptical about whether or not a particular therapy works, especially if it relies upon less orthodox and 'unseen' methods. No therapist or practitioner of complementary therapies will ever claim to 'cure' a patient alone or to replace orthodox medicine, but they would strongly support the notion that their treatments can contribute towards a feeling of well being. People who use a practitioner can expect to receive more time for treatment, a whole body approach to their problems and advice about self-help. If your relative's health is failing it is well worth considering some of these treatments as they can bring tremendous relief from distress and discomfort. Also, spending time receiving individual attention and feeling pampered is likely to help someone feel a little better in themselves.

Aromatherapy

Jill is an aromatherapist

'Aromatherapy may be used to bring about a deep sense of relaxation and well-being, reducing the negative effects of stress and anxiety.'

The ancient art of aromatherapy combines the healing properties of aromatic plant essences with massage, and is an excellent therapy to try if complementary treatments are new to you and your relative (see note of caution, page 186). It is a gentle method that encourages a relaxed feeling, and a trained therapist will ask questions first to discover the best treatment for each individual person. The complex essential oils extracted from many plants are introduced into the body where the 'life force' of the plant's essential oil can have a beneficial effect. Therapists do not claim that the oils heal directly in the sense that a synthetic drug may effect a cure; rather it is believed that the oils encourage the body to use its own natural healing forces from within. The essential oils are absorbed through the skin and pass through the tissues to the bloodstream and so travel around the body. Different combinations of oils affect different parts of the body – for example, camomile can help with digestive problems.

Jill, aromatherapist

'When buying aromatherapy oils always choose 'pure essential' oils to ensure a good quality is purchased. Labels which state 'fragrance' or 'blend' are synthetic and are useful only as mood creators or to scent a room. There are recognised retail outlets in most high streets – try good health food, body care and herbalist shops, and the larger supermarkets.'

Essential oils are extracted from plant essences by a special distillation process that changes their chemical composition. They are used in concentrations that are many times stronger than their original plant form and are rarely used undiluted because they are too powerful to use directly on the skin.

Before use essential oils should always be mixed with a carrier oil such as almond or peach. It is important to be aware that essential oils are very powerful, and that their use is not advised with people who suffer from certain conditions such as a history of miscarriage, haemophilia, advanced varicose veins or a high temperature. Always read the instructions carefully before use or follow the advice of a qualified therapist. Aromatherapy oils should never be taken by mouth.

Methods for use at home

Meg is an aromatherapist

'Try a ten minute, luxuriant aromatherapy bath, using two drops each of lavender, sandalwood and ylang-ylang pure essential oils, at the end of a day to promote a peaceful and restful night's sleep.'

The soothing oils can be used in other ways to enhance their effect:

- **Vaporization** This creates a very pleasant effect by burning oils in special containers, so that the aroma is inhaled from the air. It is believed that the healing part of the oil is breathed into the body and passes through the membranes of the lungs into the blood system. Fill the bowl with water, add 2-4 drops of your chosen oil and place a lighted night-light candle underneath. Pottery containers and blended oils are readily available in many gift shops.
- **Blending oils with other creams** This gives extra benefit for skin care to reduce dry skin and enrich hand and body creams.
- **Scented baths** Mix five drops of essential oil (such as lavender) with one tablespoon of carrier oil and add to the water to relax the body or ease aching joints.
- **Inhalation** Use in steam inhalers or place droplets on a handkerchief or pillow to bring relief from colds and catarrh.
- **Use as room fresheners** Mix two drops of essential oil in a cup of cool, boiled water and spray the air using a plant sprayer. Or mix a few drops of blended oil with pot-pourri. Or put a few droplets on to a cloth and lay it on a radiator.
- **As an aromatherapy massage** Simple massage techniques (gentler than the vigorous massages given by professional therapists), such as arm massage can easily be learned from instructions and pictures in a book.

189

For more *i*nformation

To obtain a list of qualified practitioners in your area contact one of the following organisations (see the 'Useful addresses' section, pages 202–218):

i Aromatherapy Organisation Council;

i International Federation of Aromatherapists;

i Bookshops and most libraries carry a range of suitable books on aromatherapy or ask the organisations above for a list of recommended books. It is best to use an up-to-date source as specific titles may go out of print.

Bach Flower Remedies

These Remedies are named after the medical and homeopathic trained doctor who researched the healing power of plants in the 1930s. He believed that the characteristics of disorders, whether physical or psychological, could be treated by a cure drawn from plants, sunlight, spring water and fresh air. In practice the Remedies tend to be used to treat psychological symptoms. This does not imply that the conditions are imagined, simply that they stem from whole body experiences that effect the mind as well as the body. Good examples are the conditions which cause people to feel worried, depressed, exhausted, irritable and panicky.

People have always made use of medicinal herbs, but the 38 Bach Flower Remedies claim to use the essential energy within the plant rather than actual plant material. The healing energy is stored in a preserving liquid that can be bought in a concentrated form known as the stock remedy. The concentrated forms are then diluted by mixing with pure water and an alcohol preservative. It is usual to combine several concentrates together to form the required final treatment. Because the action of Bach Remedies is mild, they cannot result in unpleasant reactions or side effects and can be used with all age groups. Although orthodox medicine cannot offer a sound reason for their claimed effects, practitioners believe that, by looking at psychological symptoms, people are encouraged to review other aspects of their behaviour, lifestyle and attitudes and this self-awareness contributes towards the healing process.

Bach Flower Remedies are available at many health shops and through especially trained therapists. They are intended primarily as a form of self-help treatment and it is therefore very easy to understand and prepare the Remedies with the help of a book. The following list gives suggestions about how the Remedies can be used. If you plan to treat yourself, you need to read about them in more depth:

■ For exhaustion and feeling drained of energy by long-standing problems, use olive.

■ For the after-effects of accident, shock, fright and grief, use star of Bethlehem.

■ For apprehension for no known reason, use aspen.

■ For tension, fear, uncontrolled and irrational thoughts, use cherry plum.

Rescue Remedy

Five of the Flower Remedies – cherry plum, clematis, impatiens, rock rose and star of Bethlehem – were combined by Dr Bach into an emergency treatment he called 'Rescue Remedy'. It can be used for a number of problems associated with shock and injury to help create a calm, soothing feeling. It can be bought as liquid or cream preparations for internal or external treatment and can be used on cuts, bites or after a traumatic experience.

For more *i*nformation

ℹ To find your nearest trained practitioner and details of publications, tapes and educational material contact the Bach Centre (see page 203).

ℹ A comprehensive book list, including *The Twelve Healers and Other Remedies* by Edward Bach, can be obtained from CW Daniel Company Ltd (address on page 207) or the Bach Centre (see page 203).

Homeopathy

Homeopathy uses tiny amounts of natural substances to enhance the body's own healing power. The practice is centuries old and is widely used as the sole form of treatment or as a complement to orthodox medicine. The name 'homeopathy' is derived from two Greek words – 'homoeos' (similar) and 'pathos' (disease). The principle is that the patient is given minute doses of a substance that, in a healthy person, would cause similar signs and symptoms to those presented by the ill person. By creating a similar condition, the homeopathic remedy stimulates the body to heal itself. The skill lies in knowing the potency of the substances and matching these to the specific signs and symptom described by the patient. Treatments are prescribed individually. Occasionally, symptoms may worsen but this is usually a short-term effect, an early stage of the healing process.

The remedies are prepared in a unique way, by repeatedly diluting plant and mineral extracts or substances that cause sensitivity (eg house dust). Unlike herbal medicine, in which only the direct effects of plants are used, homeopathic remedies are designed to treat the whole person, not just the illness, so the person's overall physical and emotional state would be assessed. There are few diseases or conditions for which homeopathy cannot be used, although there is still the need to use orthodox medical treatments. Homeopathy cannot cure what is irreversible and if long term orthodox treatments have suppressed the body's natural powers these may take a while to regenerate.

> ### *Greg (a doctor)*
>
> 'Practitioners are trained in homeopathic medicine and many also have a general medical qualification. Homeopathic medicine is available through the NHS but practitioners may not be located in all areas of the UK.'

For more *i*nformation

i To find your nearest homeopathic practitioner contact:

British Homeopathic Association (see page 204);

Society of Homeopaths (see page 216);

UK Homeopathic Medical Association (see page 217).

ⓘ To find your nearest homeopathic doctor, contact The Homeopathic Trust (see page 210).

ⓘ The organisations above will provide a booklist or use a bookshops or library.

Reflexology

Nigel suffers with depression

'I was unsure about the benefits of reflexology and about letting a therapist touch my feet as they are very sensitive. But once I got into the course it really felt helpful and she didn't hurt.'

Reflexology also complements orthodox medicine, and involves massaging reflex areas in the body, found most commonly in the feet and hands, that correspond to all parts of the body. Practitioners believe that healing is encouraged by applying pressure to these points to free blockages in energy pathways. The reflex points are laid out to form a 'map' of the body, the right and left feet reflecting the right and left sides. A reflexologist takes a full history from the person and uses both feet to give whole body treatment. It is an ideal way to boost circulation.

The method has been used for several thousand years and is described in ancient Chinese and Egyptian writings. It does not claim to cure all problems but many conditions respond well to reflexology, especially those related to stress – such as migraine, breathing disorders and circulatory and digestive problems.

To start with, the practitioner will examine the feet for signs of the primary causes of conditions, which may originate from another system of the body. Then they will move on to precise massage. This involves applying firm pressure with the thumbs to all parts of the feet that correspond to the body areas giving problems. These related areas in the foot feel especially tender when massaged and the level of tenderness indicates the degree of imbalance in the body. The skill of the reflexologist lies in their

193

ability to interpret the tenderness and apply the correct pressure, bearing in mind that some people have more sensitive feet than others. The number of treatments will vary according to the condition and the response. Reflexology is a relaxing therapy which relies on the healing power of touch rather than substances; at the end of each session people usually feel very warm and contented.

For more *i*nformation

ⓘ To find your nearest practitioner contact:

Association of Reflexologists (see page 203);

International Federation of Reflexologists (see page 211).

ⓘ The organisations above will provide a booklist, or use a bookshop or library.

Visualisation

Charles

'When my wife could no longer go out for a walk I would say to her "let's go for a walk together by the beach" and we would shut out eyes and walk for miles in our minds. It gave us so much pleasure we could almost smell the sea.'

Visualisation is a method similar to meditation but it needs much less concentration and is easier to perform. It works well whether it is done alone or with someone else. Therapists use visualisation as a healing exercise to help lift the effects of depression and to create a positive attitude towards life-threatening illnesses; it can have powerful psychological effects. It is believed that visualisation influences the brain centres that control hormone and immune systems and helps to strengthen the healing process. Using it at home is an excellent way to shut out other stressful thoughts and to mentally take yourself somewhere that induces pleasure. The technique works by creating a sense of contentment so that the brain responds to this lack of threat by telling the systems of the body to go into rest rather than alert mode. The reverse will happen if you visualise an unpleasant image. You may have noticed that if you think about a difficult situation, your body immediately responds by rousing itself for action, even though the event is imagined.

As your relative becomes more frail, and is unable to journey far, you can 'visit' a place that you have enjoyed in the past without too much effort. First, you need to sit or lie comfortably in a quiet place and decide where you want to go, then talk to your relative by giving them an imaginary 'guided' tour along familiar paths. Start and finish your journey using similar words to these: 'Close your eyes, today we will visit ... It is time to bring our journey to an end and come back home, open your eyes, gently stretch your limbs and start to think about the present.'

Other therapies

There are many other types of therapy which can be used to complement each other and orthodox medicine. You can find out more about the therapies listed below, and others, at your local library:

- **Chiropractic** This therapy relieves pain through joint manipulation
- **Herbal medicine** Herbalists use the potent healing properties of plants. Note that these preparations must always be used with caution; like all drugs, they can have unwanted (side) effects.
- **Hypnotherapy** A hypnotist will induce a trance-like state to bring about physical and mental changes.
- **Hydrotherapy** Water treatments are used to purify and heal the body.
- **Osteopathy** This is a manipulative therapy which is used widely in orthodox medicine.
- **Shiatsu** This form of massage originated in Japan. It is based on the idea that good health depends on a balanced flow of energy through specific channels in the body.
- **T'ai-chi Ch'uan** This can be described as 'meditation in motion'.

195

For more *i*nformation

The following organisations would all give you advice and supply you with further details of specialist organisations (see the 'Useful addresses' section at the end of the book) or ask at your local library:

- *i* British Holistic Medical Association (BHMA);

- *i* Centre for Study of Complementary Medicine;

- *i* Council for Complementary and Alternative Medicine;

- *i* Depression Alliance (branches in England, Scotland and Wales);

- *i* Institute of Complementary Medicine;

- *i* Institute of Optimum Nutrition;

- *i* National College of Hypnosis and Psychotherapy;

- *i* National Federation of Spiritual Healers;

- *i* No Panic;

- *i* Society for the Promotion of Nutritional Therapy;

- *i* *Readers Digest Family Guide to Alternative Medicine*, published by Reader's Digest.

- *i* *Know Your Complementary Therapies*, by Eileen Inge Herzberg, published by Age Concern Books.

Conclusion

Stress is normal in small amounts and harmful when it becomes so severe that it causes distress. The warning signs are common to everyone; however, some people because of personality type or a previous unpleasant experience react to pressure more quickly than others. The key to managing stress is learning to recognise where pressures are coming from, and then working towards changing the situation or accepting that some situations cannot be controlled.

When your body gives off the tell-tale signals that tension is rising, try to calm yourself. Slow your movements, breathe quietly and relax your muscles. Let your shoulders drop and unwind all the parts of your body that have become twisted together. Use your support systems and don't feel it is a weakness to ask for help or show signs of emotion. Crying or trembling are good ways to relieve tension but don't try to suppress the emotion as the extra effort creates more tension. Some complementary treatments provide excellent ways of relieving tension and giving yourself a reward. They should always be used alongside orthodox medicine, never as substitutes for conventional treatment.

Glossary

Antidepressants Drugs prescribed to combat depression. These can fall into a number of different catories such as *monamine oxidase inhibitors (MAOIs)* or *selective serotonin re-uptake inhibitors (SSRIs)*.

Bipolar disorder A form of mental illness which is characterised by bouts of manic and depressive episodes and very obvious mood swings.

Charters Documents that have been drawn up by healthcare trusts, social services and housing departments, in order to reflect the standards and targets that have been set to fulfil local needs.

Circadian rhythms The approximate 24-hour cycle on which many body functions governing hormone output, temperature control and appetite work.

Clinical psychologist A professionally trained person who deals with the mind and its method of working.

Cognitive impairment A technical term for mental alertness.

Computed tomography (CT) scan A method of looking at the whole body or separate parts (eg the brain) using specialist x-ray techniques.

Cortisol A substance made by the adrenal glands, found near the kidneys.

Counsellor A therapist who is trained to listen to someone in an unbiased way and help them make decisions and take practical steps towards recovery.

Cushing's syndrome A hormonal disorder resulting in the over-production of cortisol. Depression occurs frequently in this illness.

Dementia A medical term describing a range of mental states where there is mild to severe intellectual or cognitive impairment, predominantly found in older people, for example those with Alzheimer's disease or following a series of mini-strokes.

Electro-convulsive therapy (ECT) A treatment which involves passing a current of electricity through the brain, after the patient has been given a general anaesthetic and medication to relax their muscles. The treatment is usually used only when other treatments have been tried.

Electo-encephalogram (EEG) A method of reading brain patterns by means of attaching electrodes to the scalp to measure electrical wave activity in the brain.

Electrolytes Compounds which, when dissolved in water, change into electrically charged particles (ions) that can conduct electricity. An imbalance in the brain may interfere with the electrical charges transmitted between the brain cells.

Endogenous This word literally means 'coming from inside the body', so endogenous depression is likely to be caused by some form of internal trauma or malfunction, though this won't necessarily be easy to identify.

Hormones Substances made and secreted by glands in the body in order to trigger other organs into action (a form of 'chemical messenger').

Lithium/lithium carbonate A drug used to help control the mood swings found in *bipolar disorder* (see above).

Manic depressive illness Another name for *bipolar disorder* (see above).

Monamine oxidase inhibitors (MAOIs) A type of *antidepressant* drug which works by blocking an enzyme called monoamine oxidase. The enzyme is instrumental in breaking down neurotransmitters, thought to play a key role in the maintenance of mood.

Myxoedema A disease resulting from a deficiency in the hormone produced by the thyroid gland.

Neurotransmitters Chemicals in the brain that enable different parts of the brain to communicate with each other.

Noradrenaline A *neurotransmitter* (see above).

Noradrenergic and specific serotonergic antidepressants (NaS-SAs) A type of *antidepressant* drug which works by increasing levels of both serotonin and noradrenaline in the brain.

Phototherapy Treatment with a special light or light box, used for patients suffering from *SAD* (see below).

Psycho-geriatrician A psychiatrist who concentrates on working with older people with mental health problems.

Psychotherapist A professional person who is trained to treat patients with therapies that relate to their mind.

Rapid-eye movement (REM) sleep The stage of sleep when our eyes move around rapidly and we dream.

Respite care Time spent away from the person for whom a carer is responsible to enable them to take a break from the caring situation.

Seasonal affective disorder (SAD) This form of depression occurs in the winter months and appears to be caused by a reduction in daylight hours and actual sunlight.

Selective serotonin re-uptake inhibitors (SSRIs) A type of *antidepressant* drug which works by increasing levels of serotonin in the brain.

Serotonin A *neurotransmitter* (see above). It may have a function in controlling mood.

Serotonin and noradrenaline re-uptake inhibitors (SNRIs) A type of *antidepressant* drug similar to SSRIs (see above).

Sleep patterns Different stages of sleep where the deepest sleep occurs during the first part of the night, followed by more shallow sleep characterised by REM, which is repeated at regular intervals throughout the night. Both main stages of sleep are essential in human beings.

Steroid drugs The group name for compound medicines that work to reduce inflammation.

Tricyclic antidepressants (TCAs) A type of *antidepressant* drug, which is especially useful in treating physical symptoms such as sleep problems and loss of appetite.

Tyramine A substance present in the body which is also found in a wide range of foods and over-the-counter medicines. A build up of tyramine in the blood causes a dangerous increase in blood pressure level which might induce a stroke.

Useful addresses

Age Concern England
1268 London Road
London SW16 4ER
Tel: 020 8765 7200
Website: www.ageconcern.org.uk
(See page 220)

Alcohol Concern
Waterbridge House
32–36 Loman Street
London SE1 0EE
Tel: 020 7928 7377
Website: www.alcoholconcern.org.uk
Aims to raise awareness of the risk of alcohol abuse and educate people about safer drinking habits and improve existing services. Provides information only, not direct advice.

Air Transport Users Council
5th Floor, Kingsway House
103 Kingsway
London WC2B 6QX
Tel: 020 7242 3882
Website: www.caa.co.uk/anc/default.asp
Publishes a booklet 'Flight Plan', which has a section for disabled passengers.

Aromatherapy Organisation Council
PO Box 19834
London SE25 6WF
Tel: 020 8251 7912

Website: www.internethealthlibrary.com/Therapies/Aromatherapy/htm
For a list of qualified practitioners in your area.

Association of Reflexologists
27 Old Gloucester Street
London WC1N 3XX
Tel: 0870 567 3320
Website: www.aor.org.uk
For names of reflexologists.

Association to Aid the Sexual and Personal Relationships of the Disabled
58 Knebworth Avenue
London E17 5AJ
Tel: 020 8527 7648
Website: www.spod-uk.org
Promotes the preservation and protection of health, and the relief of distress and sickness – particularly with regard to personal relationship issues – of people with a disability.

Bach Centre
Mount Vernon Ltd
Bakers Lane
Sotwell
Wallingford
Oxfordshire OX10 0PX
Tel: 01491 834678
Website: www.bachcentre.com/centre
For list of trained practitioners and details of publications, tapes and educational material.

British Association for Counselling and Psychotherapy
1 Regent Place
Rugby
Warwickshire CV21 2PJ
Helpline: 0870 443 5252
Website: www.bacp.co.uk
Publishes a directory of counsellors and psychotherapists in the UK.

British Complementary Medicine Association (BCMA)
249 Fosse Road South
Leicester LE3 1AE
Tel: 0116 282 5511
Website: www.bcma.co.uk
Publishes BCMA National Practitioner Register listing practitioners who belong to member organisations.

British Herbal Medicine Association (BHMA)
Sun House
Church Street
Stroud
Gloucestershire GL5 1JL
Tel: 01453 751389
Website: www.bhma.info
Provides an information service and list of qualified herbal practitioners.

British Holistic Medical Association (BHMA)
59 Lansdowne Place
Hove
East Sussex BN3 1FL
Tel: 01273 725951
Website: www.bhma-sec.dircon.co.uk
For directory of members and book/tape list.

British Homeopathic Association (BHA)
Hahneman House
29 Park Street West
Luton LU1 3BE
Tel: 08704 443950
www.trust.homeopathy.org
Provides an information service, newsletter, book list and names of homeopathic practitioners.

BNA (British Nursing Association)
North Place
82 Great North Road
Hatfield
Hertfordshire AL9 5BL

Tel: 01707 263544
Website: www.bnauk.com
For respite and nursing care.

British Red Cross
9 Grosvenor Crescent
London SW1X 7EJ
Tel: 020 7235 5454
Or look in the telephone directory for a local contact number.
For advice about arranging for equipment on loan.

Care and Repair England
3rd Floor
Bridgford House
Pavilion Road
West Bridgford
Nottingham NG2 5GJ
Tel: 0115 982 1527
Website: www.careandrepair.england.org.uk
Advice and practical assistance to older and disabled people and those on low incomes, to help them improve their home conditions.

Carers UK
20–25 Glasshouse Yard
London EC1A 4JS
Tel: 020 7490 8818
CarersLine: 0808 808 7777
Website: www.carersonline.org.uk
Acts as the national voice of carers, raising awareness and providing support, information and advice.

Centre for Study of Complementary Medicine
51 Bedford Place
Southampton SO15 2DT
Tel: 023 8033 4752
For advice and details of specialist organisations.

Community Transport Association
Highbank
Halton Street
Hyde
Cheshire SK14 2NY
Tel: 0161 351 1475
Advice: 0161 367 8780
Services to benefit providers of transport for people with mobility problems. Also keeps a database of all Dial-a-Ride schemes.

Consumers' Association
2 Marylebone Road
London NW1 4DF
Tel: 020 7770 7000
Website: www.which.net
Represents the consumer interest and campaigns for improvements in goods and services.

Council for Complementary and Alternative Medicine (CCAM)
63 Jeddo Road
London W12 6HQ
Tel: 020 7724 9103
Advice and details of specialist organisations.

Counsel and Care
Lower Ground Floor
Twyman House
16 Bonny Street
London NW1 9PG
Tel: 020 7485 1566
Website: www.counselandcare.org.uk
Offers free counselling, information and advice for older people and carers, including specialist advice about using independent agencies and the administration of trust funds for single payments (eg respite care).

Crossroads Care
10 Regent Place
Rugby
Warwickshire CV21 2PN
Tel: 01788 573653
Website: www.crossroads.org.uk
For a range of services, including personal and respite care.

Cruse – Bereavement Care
126 Sheen Road
Richmond
Surrey TW9 1UR
Tel: 020 8940 4818
Website: www.crusebereavementcare.org.uk
For all types of bereavement counselling and a wide range of publications.

CW Daniel Company Ltd
1 Church Path
Saffron Walden
Essex CB10 1JP

Depression Alliance (England)
35 Westminster Bridge Road
London SE1 7JB
Tel: 020 7633 0557
Textphone: 020 7928 9992
Website: www.depressionalliance.org
Provides information, support and understanding to everyone affected by depression and campaigns to raise awareness of the illness.

Depression Alliance (Scotland)
3 Grosvenor Gardens
Edinburgh EH12 5JU
Tel: 0131 467 3050

Depression Alliance (Cymru)
11 Plas Melin
Westbourne Road
Whitchurch
Cardiff CF4 2BT
Tel: 029 2069 2891

Dial-a-Ride (DART)
See Community Transport Scheme (above).

Disabled Living Centres Council
Redbank House
4 St Chads Street
Manchester M8 8QA
Tel: 0161 834 1044
Website: www.dlcc.org.uk
For Disabled Living Centre nearest you, where you can see aids and equipment.

Disabled Living Foundation
380–384 Harrow Road
London W9 2HU
Tel: 020 7289 6111
Equipment helpline: 0870 603 9177
Minicom: 0879 603 9176
Website: www.dlf.org.uk
Information and advice about all aspects of daily living (and aids) for people with disability.

Disabled Persons Railcard Office
PO Box 1YT
Newcastle-upon-Tyne NE99 1YT
Helpline: 0191 269 0303
For railcard offering concessionary fares. An application form and useful booklet called Rail Travel for Disabled Passengers can be found at most larger stations or from address above.

Drinkline
7th Floor, Weddell House
13–14 Smithfield
London EC1A 9DL
Tel: 020 7332 0202
National Alcohol helpline that provides confidential information, help and advice about drinking to anyone, including people worried about someone else's drinking.

Elderly Accommodation Counsel
3rd Floor
89 Albert Embankment
London SE1 7TP
Tel: 020 7820 1343
Fax: 020 7820 3970
Email: enquiries@e-a-c.demon.co.uk
Website: www.housingcare.org
Computerised information about all forms of accommodation for older people (including nursing homes and hospices) and advice on top-up funding.

EXTEND
22 Maltings Drive
Wheathampstead
Hertfordshire AL4 8QJ
Tel/Fax: 01582 832760
Provides exercise in the form of movement to music for people over 60 years and less able people of all ages.

Federation of Independent Advice Centres
4 Dean's Court
St Paul's Churchyard
London EC4V 5AA
Tel: 020 7489 1800
Promotes the provision of independent advice services in the UK.

Help the Aged
207–221 Pentonville Road
London N19 UZ
Tel: 020 7278 1114
Fax: 020 7278 1116
Email: info@helptheaged.org.uk
Website: www.helptheaged.org.uk
Advice and support for older people and their carers.

HELPBOX
The Help for Health Trust
Freepost
Winchester SO22 5BR
Tel: 01962 849100
A computer database that holds a vast and comprehensive range of health-related information.

Holiday Care Service
7th Floor, Sunley House
4 Bedford Park
Croydon
Surrey CR0 2AP
Tel: 0845 124 9971
Textphone: 0845 124 9976
Fax: 0845 124 9972
Email: holiday.care@virgin.net
Website: www.holidaycare.org.uk
Information and advice on holidays, travel facilities and respite care available for people with disabilities, on low income or with special needs.

Homeopathic Trust
2 Powis Place
Great Ormond Street
London WC1N 3HT
Tel: 020 7837 9469
For the names of homeopathic trained doctors.

Independent Healthcare Association
22 Little Russell Street
London WC1A 2HT
Tel: 020 7430 0837
Website: www.iha.org.uk
For information about finding and paying for residential and nursing home care.

Institute of Complementary Medicine (ICM)
PO Box 194
London SE16 7QZ
Tel: 020 7237 5165
Advice and details of specialist organisations.

Institute of Optimum Nutrition
5 Jerdan Place
Fulham
London SW6 1BE

International Federation of Aromatherapists
182 Chiswick High Road
London W4 1PP
Tel: 020 8742 2605
For a book list and details of qualified practitioners in your area.

International Federation of Reflexologists
78 Edridge Road
Croydon
Surrey CR0 1EF
Tel: 020 8667 9454
For names of qualified reflexologists in your area.

International Society of Aromatherapists
ISPA House
82 Ashby Road
Hinckley
Leicestershire LE10 1SN
Tel: 01455 637987
For a book list and details of qualified practitioners in your area.

Jewish Care
Stewart Young House
221 Golders Green Road
London NW11 9DQ
Tel: 020 8458 3282
Social care, personal support and residential homes for Jewish people.

The Manic Depression Fellowship
Castle Works
21 St Georges Road
London SE1 6ES
Tel: 020 7793 2600 (England)
Tel: 0141 400 1867 (Scotland)
Tel: 01633 244244 (Wales)
Offers information and advice specifically about Manic Depression/Bipolar Disorder.

MIND (National Association for Mental Health)
Granta House
15–19 Broadway
London E15 4BQ
Tel: 0847 660 163 (Monday–Friday, 9.15am–4.45pm)
Website: www.mind.org.uk
Information service for all matters relating to mental health.

MIND Cymru
23 St Mary's Street
Cardiff CF1 2AA
Tel: 029 2039 5123

Motability
Gate House, West Gate
Harlow
Essex CM20 1HR
Helpline: 01279 635666
Advice about cars, scooters and wheelchairs for disabled people.

National Association of Councils for Voluntary Service
3rd Floor, Arundel Court
177 Arundel Street
Sheffield S1 2NU
Tel: 0114 278 6636
Promotes and supports the work of councils for voluntary service.

National College of Hypnosis and Psychotherapy
12 Cross Street
Nelson
Lancashire BB9 7EN
Tel: 01282 699378
Publishes an annual directory of practitioners.

National Federation of Spiritual Healers
Old Manor Farm Studio
Church Street
Sunbury on Thames
Middlesex TW16 6RG
Tel: 0891 616080 (premium rate line)
Advice and details of spiritual healers.

New World Aurora
16A Neal's Yard
Covent Garden
London WC2H 9DP
Tel: 020 7379 5972
For catalogue of relaxation music tapes.

NHS Direct
Tel: 0845 46 47
Website: www.nhsdirect.nhs.uk
A 24-hour nurse-led helpline providing confidential health-care advice and information.

No Panic
Tel: 0800 783 1531
Telephone service only for an information pack about dealing with anxiety and panic. Callers are asked to leave details of their name and address on an answerphone as the organisation cannot return calls.

212

Northern Ireland Association for Mental Health
80 University Street
Belfast BT7 1HE
Tel: 028 9032 8474
A voluntary organisation providing services for people with mental health needs, including residential and day care, counselling, information, education and training.

Public Guardianship Office
Protection Division
Archway Tower
2 Junction Road
London N19 5SZ
Tel: 020 7664 7300/7000
Enquiry Line: 0845 330 2900
Advice about powers of attorney.

Quitline
Tel: 0800 002 200
A freephone helpline that provides confidential and practical advice for people wanting to give up smoking.

RADAR (Royal Association for Disability and Rehabilitation)
12 City Forum
250 City Road
London EC1V 8AF
Tel: 020 7250 3222
Information about aids and mobility, holidays and leisure.

Relate
Herbert Gray College
Little Church Street
Rugby
Warwickshire CV21 3AP
Tel: 01788 573241
Helpline: 0845 130 4010
Counselling and help with relationship difficulties.

Research Institute for Consumer Affairs (RICA)
2 Marylebone Road
London NW1 4DF
Tel: 020 7830 7679
Tests and evaluates goods and services for disabled and older people, including ordinary consumer products as well as special aids and equipment.

Royal College of Psychiatrists
12 Belgrave Square
London SW1X 8PG
Tel: 020 7235 2351
Publishes a range of information for dealing with anxieties, phobias, depression and bereavement.

SADA (Seasonal Affective Disorder Association)
PO Box 989
Steyning BN44 3HG
Tel: 01903 814942
Offers information, advice and support for people with seasonal affective disorder, including the sale of light boxes.

The Samaritans
46 Marshall Street
London W1V 1LR
Tel: 08457 90 90 90
Textphone: 08457 90 91 92 (24 hours every day)
Offers confidential emotional support to any person who is suicidal or despairing.

The Scottish Association for Mental Health
Cumbrae House
15 Carlton Court
Glasgow G5 9JP
Tel: 0141 568 7000
Offers confidential support, information and advice to any person suffering from a mental health illness, including other people affected by the illness.

St John Ambulance
Look in the telephone directory for local contact number.
For advice about arranging equipment on loan and first aid courses.

Society of Homeopaths
4A Artizan Road
Northampton NN1 4HU
Tel: 01604 621400
For names of homeopathic practitioners.

Society for the Promotion of Nutritional Therapy
1st Floor
Enterprise Centre
Eastbourne
East Sussex BN21 1BE

Sports Council
16 Upper Woburn Place
London WC1H 0QP
Tel: 020 7263 1500
Provides general information about all sports.

Stress Management Training Institute
Foxhills
30 Victoria Avenue
Shanklin
Isle of Wight PO37 6LS
Tel: 01983 868166
Publishes a wide range of materials to help reduce stress: leaflets, audio tapes, books and newsletter.

Survivors Speak Out
34 Osnaburgh Street
London NW1 3ND
Tel: 020 7916 5472
A national campaigning group of survivors of mental health services which campaigns for better treatment for people with mental health problems and provides advice and information.

Tripscope
The Vassall Centre
Gill Avenue
Bristol BS16 2QQ
Tel/Textphone: 08457 585641
A national travel and transport information service for older and disabled people.

UK College of Complementary Health Care Studies
St Charles Hospital
Exmoor Street
London W10 6DZ
Tel: 020 8964 1205
For a list of qualified practitioners of therapeutic massage.

UK Homeopathic Medical Association
6 Livingstone Road
Gravesend
Kent DA12 5DZ
Tel: 01474 560336
For the names of homeopathic practitioners.

United Kingdom Home Care Association (UKHCA)
42B Banstead Road
Carshalton Beeches
Surrey SM5 3NW
Tel: 020 8288 1551
For information about organisations providing home care in your area.

University of the Third Age (U3A)
National Office
26 Harrison Street
London WC1H 8JG
Tel: 020 7837 8838
Day-time study and recreational classes. Send a sae for further information about classes for older people, or look in the telephone directory for local branch.

Vehicle Excise Duty (Road Tax)
DLA Unit
Warbreck House
Warbreck Hill Road
Blackpool FY2 0YE
Tel: 08457 123456
Information about exemption from road tax for vehicles used exclusively by or for disabled people.

Volunteer Development England
(Formerly National Association of Volunteer Bureaux)
New Oxford House
16 Waterloo Street
Birmingham B2 5UG
Tel: 0121 633 4555
Information on matters related to volunteering, with a directory of volunteer bureaux and other publications.

Winged Fellowship Trust
Angel House
20–32 Pentonville Road
London N1 9XD
Tel: 020 7833 2594
Website: www.wft.org.uk
Provides respite care and holidays for physically disabled people, with or without a partner.

About Depression Alliance

Depression Alliance is the leading UK charity for people with depression.

The charity works to relieve and to prevent this treatable condition by providing information, support and understanding to those who are affected by it. It also campaigns to raise awareness amongst the general public about the realities of depression.

A member-led organisation, Depression Alliance has offices in England, Scotland and Wales. It co-ordinates a national network of self-help groups so that people with depression can share experiences and coping strategies with others in similar situations. Depression Alliance produces a unique series of free publications which provide information on depression and related topics. A range of mutual support services for members are also offered. These include a 'pen friend' scheme, correspondence service and email group.

Depression Alliance
35 Westminster Bridge Road
London SE1 7JB
Tel: 020 7633 0557
Website: www.depressionalliance.org.uk

About Age Concern

Caring for someone with depression is one of a wide range of publications produced by Age Concern England, the National Council on Ageing. Age Concern works on behalf of all older people and believes later life should be fulfilling and enjoyable. For too many this is impossible. As the leading charitable movement in the UK concerned with ageing and older people, Age Concern finds effective ways to change that situation.

Where possible, we enable older people to solve problems themselves, providing as much or as little support as they need. A network of local Age Concerns, supported by many thousands of volunteers, provides community-based services such as lunch clubs, day centres and home visiting.

Nationally, we take a lead role in campaigning, parliamentary work, policy analysis, research, specialist information and advice provision, and publishing. Innovative programmes promote healthier lifestyles and provide older people with opportunities to give the experience of a lifetime back to their communities.

Age Concern is dependent on donations, covenants and legacies.

Age Concern England
1268 London Road
London SW16 4ER
Tel: 020 8765 7200
Fax: 020 8765 7211
Website:
www.ageconcern.org.uk

Age Concern Scotland
113 Rose Street
Edinburgh EH2 3DT
Tel: 0131 220 3345
Fax: 0131 220 2779
Website:
www.ageconcernscotland.org.uk

Age Concern Cymru
4th Floor
1 Cathedral Road
Cardiff CF11 9SD
Tel: 029 2037 1566
Fax: 029 2039 9562
Website: www.accymru.org.uk

Age Concern Northern Ireland
3 Lower Crescent
Belfast BT7 1NR
Tel: 028 9024 5729
Fax: 028 9023 5497
Website: www.ageconcernni.org

Other books in this series

The Carers Handbook series has been written for the families and friends of older people. It guides readers through key care situations and aims to help readers make informed, practical decisions. All the books in the series:

- are packed full of detailed advice and information;
- offer step-by-step guidance on the decisions which need to be taken;
- examine all the options available;
- are full of practical checklists and case studies;
- point you towards specialist help;
- guide you through the social services maze;
- are fully up to date with recent guidelines and issues;
- draw on Age Concern's wealth of experience.

Caring for someone with an alcohol problem
Mike Ward
£6.99   0-86242-372-4

Caring for someone with arthritis
Jim Pollard
£6.99   0-86242-373-2

Caring for someone with cancer
Toni Battison
£6.99   0-86242-382-1

Caring for someone with dementia
Jane Brotchie
£6.99   0-86242-368-6

Caring for someone with diabetes
Marina Lewycka
£6.99   0-86242-374-0

Caring for someone at a distance
Julie Spencer-Cingöz
£6.99 0-86242-367-8

Caring for someone who is dying
Penny Mares
£6.99 0-86242-370-8

Caring for someone with hearing loss
Marina Lewycka
£6.99 0-86242-380-5

Caring for someone with a heart problem
Toni Battison
£6.99 0-86242-371-6

Caring for someone with sight problem
Marina Lewycka
£6.99 0-86242-381-3

Caring for someone who has had a stroke
Philip Coyne with Penny Mares
£6.99 0-86242-369-4

Choices for the carer of an elderly relative
Marina Lewycka
£6.99 0-86242-375-9

The Carer's Handbook: What to do and who to turn to
Marina Lewycka
£6.99 0-86242-366-X

Publications from Age Concern Books

Your Rights: A guide to money benefits for older people
Sally West

A highly acclaimed annual guide to the State benefits available to older people. It contains current information on Income Support, Housing Benefit and retirement pensions, among other matters, and provides advice on how to claim.

For more information, please telephone 0870 44 22 120

Know Your Complementary Therapies
Eileen Inge Herzberg

People who practise natural medicine have many different ideas and philosophies, but they all share a common basic belief: that we can all heal ourselves – we just need a little help from time to time.

Written in clear, jargon-free language, the book provides an introduction to complementary therapies, including acupuncture, herbal medicine, aromatherapy, homeopathy and osteopathy. Uniquely focusing on complementary therapies and older people, the book helps readers to decide which therapies are best suited to their needs, and where to go for help.

£9.99 0-86242-309-0

If you would like to order any of these titles, please write to the address below, enclosing a cheque or money order for the appropriate amount (plus £1.95 p&p) made payable to Age Concern England. Credit card orders may be made on 0870 44 22 120.

Age Concern Books
Units 5 and 6
Industrial Estate
Brecon
Powys LD3 8LA

Bulk order discounts

Age Concern Books is pleased to offer a discount on orders totalling 50 or more copies of the same title. For details, please contact Age Concern Books on Tel: 0870 44 22 120.

Customised editions

Age Concern Books is pleased to offer a free 'customisation' service for anyone wishing to purchase 500 or more copies of the title. This gives you the option to have a unique front cover design featuring your organisation's logo and corporate colours, or adding your logo to the current cover design. You can also insert an additional four pages of text for a small additional fee. Existing clients include many of the biggest names in British industry, retailing and finance, the Trades Union Movement, educational establishments, the statutory and voluntary sectors, and welfare associations. **For full details, please contact Sue Henning, Age Concern Books, Astral House, 1268 London Road, London SW16 4ER. Fax: 020 8765 7211. Email: hennings@ace.org.uk**

Visit our Website at www.ageconcern.org.uk/shop

Age Concern Information Line/ Factsheets subscription

Age Concern produces 44 comprehensive factsheets designed to answer many of the questions older people (or those advising them) may have. Topics covered include money and benefits, health, community care, leisure and education, and housing. For up to five free factsheets, telephone 0800 00 99 66 (7am-7pm, seven days a week, every day of the year). Alternatively you may prefer to write to Age Concern, FREEPOST (SWB 30375), ASBUR-TON, Devon TQ13 7ZZ.

For professionals working with older people, the factsheets are available on an annual subscription service, which includes updates throughout the year. For further details and costs of the subscription, please write to Age Concern England at the above Freepost address.

We hope that this publication has been useful to you. If so, we would very much like to hear from you. Alternatively, if you feel that we could add or change anything, then please write and tell us, using the following Freepost address: Age Concern, FREEPOST CN1794, London SW16 4BR.

Index